Sorry...

Saying sorry

Prof 114 Elève 99

Read the text

Match

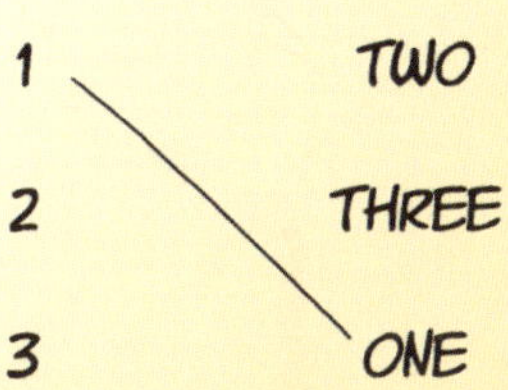

Tick

Teacher's instructions

Prof 115 Elève 100

Now it's your turn, play "Simon says ...» with your class!

hatier-clic.fr/21PYB00a

Time to pronounce!

Familiarise-toi avec les sons des mots suivants. Ils te serviront de référence toute l'année. En parlant anglais, tu vas même découvrir des sons qui n'existent pas en français.

Version imprimable
hatier-clic.fr/21PYB00b

VOYELLES

Audio Prof 116 Elève 101

iː	ɪ	e
ch**ee**ks	f**i**sh and ch**i**ps	**e**gg

ɔː	ɒ	ə
c**o**rgi	cl**o**ck	fam**i**ly

ɜː	ʊ	uː
the w**or**ld	the w**oo**ds	s**u**perhero

æ	ɑː	ʌ
apple	gl**a**sses	d**ou**ble-decker b**u**s

DIPHTONGUES

Audio Prof 117 Elève 102

ɪə	eə
ear	sc**are**d

ʊə	eɪ
t**our**	l**a**ser

aɪ	ɔɪ
island	t**oy**s

əʊ	aʊ
gh**o**st	m**ou**th

CONSONNES

Audio Prof 118 Elève 103

ʃ	tʃ	h
(pencil) **sh**arpener	**ch**ocolate	**h**ouse

θ	ð	ʒ
bir**th**day	clo**th**es	trea**s**ure

dʒ	ŋ	j
bri**dge**	E**ng**lish	(Happy) **New Year**

1. Listen to the audio and point to the word you hear. Repeat it!
2. **GROUP WORK** Practice repeating the words.
3. Play games. **WB > P. 6**

PACK *your* BAGS 6e A1 > A2

DIRECTION D'OUVRAGE

ELISABETH JARDON
Inspectrice Ac. Créteil (77, 93, 94)

AUTEURE ET CONSEIL NUMÉRIQUE

MELANIE AURIEL
Chargée de mission Collège Numérique 56

AUTEUR·E·S

REGINE BALLONAD-BERTHOIS
Collège Léonard de Vinci, Saint-Brieuc (22)

HOWARD BENNETT
Collège Lubet Barbon, St Pierre du Mont (40)

ISABELLE DEJARDIN
Collège Saint Blaise, Vertou (44)

MOLLY EASTAFF
Collège Liberté, Drancy (93)

ÉLISE FOLLET
Collège Marie Curie, Les Lilas (93)

MARIE GOURVES
Collège de Kerdurand, Riantec (56)

SYLVIE MALENFANT
Collège du Fort, Sucy-en-Brie (94)

SANDRA SITBON
Collège André Malraux, Louvres (95)

Hatier

Beaucoup d'enseignant·e·s ont donné leur avis sur ce manuel à plusieurs étapes de son élaboration en participant aux différentes études. Cette démarche constructive nous a permis de faire évoluer le projet pour qu'il corresponde au mieux à vos besoins et pratiques en classe avec vos élèves. Nous les remercions tous chaleureusement notamment :

Elise Brassier, *Tassin La Demi Lune* / Fabien Cappe, *Saint Nicolas de Port* / Sophie Rieunier, *La Farlède* / Marie-Cecile Gilbert, *Aigre* / Serra Berhouma, *Persan* / Guillaume Bricard, *St Pierre des Corps* / Philomène Fernandes, Créteil / Pauline Roux, *Saint Yzan de soudiac* / Sophie Laverdure, *Olivet* / Dorothée Cantagrel, *Velizy Villacoublay* / Sebastien Cellier, *Limay* / Dorothee Landais, *Rueil Malmaison* / Anne-Laure Molina, *Paris* / Nicole Selme, *Soisy sous Montmorency* / Alice-Eva Molineus, *Rocbaron* / Sandrine Moreau, *Secondigny* / Sandrine Gau, *Poix du nord* / Charlotte Bourgeon, *Nice* / Sophie Gal, *Poissy* / Ghislain Lesauvage, *Toulon* / Océane Deshayes-Ducoffre, *Vertus* / Antonina Wiewiorka, *St Romain de Colbosc* / Faustine Castillo, *Perpignan* / Virginie Jousset, *Pau* / Laure Friant, *Neuilly sur Seine* / Sophie Mead, *Thionville* / Elodie Guégan, *Annecy* / Geraldine Malrieu, *Carcassonne* / Sabrina Larrieu - Di Monda, *Saint Affrique* / Fabienne Le Floch, *Othis* / Selma Southgate, *Payroux* / Sandie Merlevede, *Bethune* / Pauline Ciseran, *Thieux* / Audrey Boutelière, *Béziers* / Melanie Rivage, *Cahors* / Muriel Schroeder, *Foix* / Elodie Granger, *La Tour du Pin* / Amandine Lelong, *Isigny sur Mer* / Salomé Thevenoux, *Savouges* / Marjorie Léon, *Clermont l'Hérault* / Marie-Ange Marmillon, *Villers-Bocage* / Carole Jeanne, *Reyrieux* / Jennifer Mencarelli, *Lexy* / Marie-laure Boivin, *Pouancé* / Sandrine Labrousse, *Limoges* / Laura Ferrer-Guillaume, *Gennevilliers* / Clotilde Viart, *Cergy* / Juliette Crosnier, *Evreux* / Ludovic Prouveur, *Denain* / Sarah Zugmeyer, *Pont-Saint-Esprit* / Bénédicte Albert-Cufi, *Bénédicte* / Caroline Bouj, *Paris* / Alexia Roberts, *Pontgibaud* / Céline Chabanne, *Tours* / Cécile Asquini, *Lyon* / Lindsay Broohm, *Villeneuve-lès-Avignon* / Christine Marchi, *Larra* / Sabrina Creuzet, *St Pourçain sur Sioule* / Carole Weber, *Mourmelon le Grand* / Delphine Moulenat-Batlle, *Cabestany* / Coralie Girault, *Méru* / Sophie Lovergne, *Abbeville* / Sophie Morionnet-Sanchez, *Saint Paul-Lès-Dax* / Nancy Militao, *Bailleul* / Stéphanie Vallot, *Villeurbanne* / David Clement, *Orléans* / Keltoum Beldjilali, *Lyon* / Sylvie Mercier, *Roquebrune Sur Argens* / Philippe Margarito, *Montrevel-en-Bresse* / Frédérique Giusto, *Salon de Provence* / Caroline Morin, *Plérin* / Angélique Medard, *Le Mans* / Claudine Moulène, *Biarritz* / Ségolène Bernier, *Lannion* / Emeline Ely, *Saint-Louis* / Sébastien Soignier, *Monaco* / Mélodie Guillouët, *Bellegarde* / Nathalie de Fuisseaux, *Poitiers* / Charles Dengpheng, *Levallois Perret* / Déborah Heuzé, *Brionne* / Héritier Losembe, *Kinshasa* / Christine Laforge, *Saint-Denis* / Bruno Bitoun, *Hem* / Adeline Paget, *La Norville* / Sigrid Yvin, *Bogotà* / Caroline Andrieux, *Gerzat* / Céline Cezard, *Annecy* / Nelly Lancelot, *Pont-Scorff* / Gaëlle Mas, *Saint-Lô* / Caroline Francois, *Saint Etienne du Rouvray* / Athalie Ange, *Rosny-sous-bois* / Sylvie Druelle, *Saultain* / Gaëlle Markowski-Deriot, *Le Creusot* / France Rigouste, *Aussonne* / Astrid Cassar, *Lésigny* / Océane Verscheure, *St Bonnet le Château* / Delphine Davin, *Saint Bonnet en Champsaur* / Laurence Sery, *Le Tampon* / Marie Lestage, *La Brede* / Noémie Cora, *Dunkerque* / Ahlam Aissa, *Lyon* / Anne-Lyse Luc, *St Etienne* / Mylène Sobczyk Girerd, *Bourgoin Jallieu* / Christine Bonthoux, *Villard de Lans* / Sandrine Vezilier, *Chaumont-en-Vexin* / Sylvie Laporte, *Amiens* / Virginie Le Coadou, *Plougrescant* / Véronique Médana, *Cadaujac* / Valérie Boisnard, *Cormeilles en Parisis* / Rachael Harris, *Geneve* / Didier Blanchais, *Courdimanche* / Estelle Fournier Biernacki, *Arras* / Jeremy Nowak, *Loriol* / Sophie Flandre, *St Georges de Reneins* / Cyrine Ismail, *Marseille* / Claude Grychta, *Billom Puy de Dôme* / Jeremy Colart, *Froissy* / Nadia Auffret, *Liverdun* / Sylviane Rougier, *Clermont Ferrand* / Christine Karpe, *Sables d'Olonne* / Maëva Béguin-Way, *Béziers* / Blandine Gillet, *Grenoble* / Lisa Miquerol, *Toulouse* / Audrey Vidal, *Montrouge* / Philippe Chaubard, *Paris* / Isabelle Boresy, *Amiens* / Corinne Chandler, *Gacé* / Elise Rossi, *Nouméa* / Estelle Loubet, *St Sulpice la Pointe* / Annie Argelas, *Courthézon* / Sonia Marchadé, *Bédarieux* / Anne-France Mahabirsingh, *Mapou* / Anne Pinot-Busson, *Le Mans* / Delphine Roulleau, *Redon* / Alix Zenier, *Nancy*

Les auteur·e·s tiennent à remercier l'équipe Hatier et en particulier leurs éditeurs et éditrices :
Magomed Bogolov, Sean Demoranville, Joëlle Dejonckère et Anke Feuchter.

Conception graphique : Primo & Primo
Adaptation et mise en pages : Gudrun Challe
Édition : Magomed Bogolov, Joëlle Dejonckère, Sean Demoranville
Illustrations : Vincent Brascaglia, Anne-Olivia Messana, Mathieu de Muizon, Yllya, Marie-Hélène Van Tilbeurgh
Cartographie : Légendes Cartographie, L'atelier Cartographik
Droits : Andrea Freire

ISBN : 978-2-401-07721-8

AVANT-PROPOS

Chère et cher collègue,

Conforme au dernier programme du Cycle 3, votre manuel et ses outils s'appuient sur des axes forts et qui répondent à vos attentes.

Un ancrage culturel authentique

Sur la thématique motivante du voyage, ce manuel privilégie l'ancrage culturel en s'appuyant sur des documents authentiques et variés. Le développement de la compétence culturelle et des divers parcours d'éducation permet aux élèves de dépasser les stéréotypes et les clichés, par une meilleure connaissance de l'autre.

Des thématiques motivantes et d'actualité

Afin d'entrer en douceur au collège, une chasse au trésor emmène l'élève dans un rebrassage ludique des acquis du primaire.
Ensuite, les *Trips* se déclinent chacun en deux *Quests*. Vous y trouverez des thématiques originales, d'autres plus habituelles mais toujours abordées de manière à renouveler l'intérêt de l'élève… et de l'enseignant·e !

Une approche pédagogique actionnelle

Pour pouvoir réaliser la tâche finale (*Time to act*) et faire aboutir les apprentissages, les *Quests* privilégient le travail des cinq activités langagières, plaçant chaque élève en situation d'acteur. De très nombreux documents authentiques (vidéos, *comics*, tableaux, *leaflets*, chansons, etc.) sont abordés de façon à privilégier la réflexion et le développement des compétences. En fin de *Quest*, après des étapes réflexives, culturelles et ludiques, la page *Time to check* engage l'élève à s'autoévaluer, avant d'aborder *Time to act*. C'est un moment privilégié pour faire le point sur ses apprentissages et apporter réellement de la remédiation.
Une fois la tâche réalisée, un passeport numérique ou papier valide les compétences des élèves acquises dans le *Trip*.

Un apprentissage contextualisé, personnalisé et spiralaire

Au fil de chaque *Quest*, l'étude de la langue entraîne la réactivation des acquis et la manipulation langagière, pour une meilleure mémorisation. Des activités et exercices lexicaux et phonologiques visent une langue actuelle et quotidienne. Ces situations de communication concrètes privilégient l'interaction, l'écoute de l'autre pour coopérer. Afin d'accompagner l'élève, des parcours différenciés plus ou moins guidés dans le cahier d'activités encouragent et valorisent ses progrès. Des conseils méthodologiques dispensés par un sympathique petit bulldog émaillent les pages du manuel, pour doter chaque élève de stratégies de réception et de production.

Des outils numériques pour les enseignants et pour les élèves

En lien avec le contenu des *Quests*, nous avons développé des exercices de remédiation en ligne, des *escape games*, de nombreuses animations grammaticales et des présentations interactives et ludiques à utiliser en classe ou à la maison, pour varier sans se lasser.
Des alternatives numériques sont systématiquement proposées pour chaque tâche finale, pour la rendre encore plus motivante.

Pack your bags and … let's go!

Petite note aux parents

L'entrée au collège

Ce manuel a été conçu pour votre enfant, afin d'entrer en douceur au collège. Un premier voyage sur le mode des *serious games* lui permettra de réactiver les acquis du primaire. Soyez rassurés, si votre enfant n'a pas eu l'opportunité d'étudier l'anglais avant son entrée en collège, il pourra facilement développer ces apprentissages.

Pour accompagner votre enfant au quotidien

S'entraîner en ligne
Des exercices d'entrainement et de révision autocorrectifs sont disponibles depuis la maison via des mini-URLS, pour travailler l'oral, la grammaire et le vocabulaire.

Acquérir les bons réflexes
Un petit bulldog attachant dispensera des conseils méthodologiques qui donneront à votre enfant des stratégies pour mieux apprendre et comprendre.

Privilégier l'écoute
Des enregistrements sonores vous offriront la possibilité d'accompagner votre enfant. Rendez-vous sur https://langues-eleves.editions-hatier.fr/ pour télécharger les MP3.

Starting up

Trip 9 Be fantastic, use less plastic!

Trip 10 Little Inventors

N'oublie pas les aides dont tu disposes pour bien voyager dans ton année d'anglais !

Dans les annexes du manuel

Ton lexique illustré … avec plus de **10 planches** pour poursuivre les aventures d'Amy et Keanu en révisant le vocabulaire de ton année.

Tout ce que tu veux savoir sur *Halloween, Thanksgiving, Christmas* et *Saint Patrick's Day* … avec des **animations interactives** pour en savoir plus et des activités à télécharger !

Dans ton *workbook*

Le *workbook* est là pour t'aider en classe et à la maison !

Tous les voyageurs doivent se préparer avant de partir. C'est l'objectif de la rubrique « ***Do you remember*** » en début de chaque leçon.

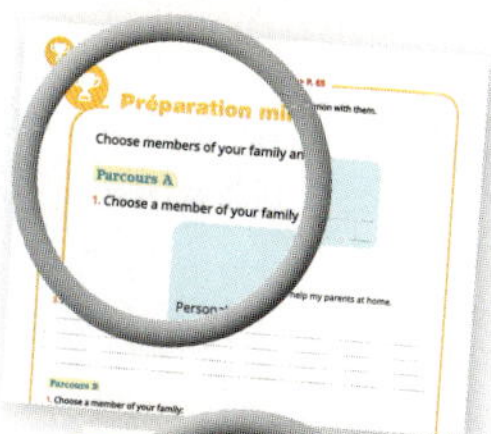

Pour arriver à destination, il faut savoir se ménager. Ton ***workbook*** propose des activités de difficultés graduées pour faire le chemin à ton rythme.

À chaque étape, ton projet avance. Ton ***workbook*** détaille les challenges qui te sont proposés pour t'accompagner au mieux dans leur réalisation.

Prends ton temps aussi pour profiter au maximum de ce que tu apprends ! Ton ***workbook*** t'aidera à retenir les règles de grammaire en les reformulant toi-même !

Le carnet de bord du voyageur !
Ton ***workbook***, c'est aussi l'endroit où tu vas collecter tes badges et enregistrer tes progrès !

The road to success!

Pour t'aider, pour t'amuser, pour mesurer tes progrès, retrouve tout au long de ton manuel des outils en ligne en accès gratuit !

En ouverture…

… **3 escape games** pour rythmer ton année

Avec les règles de grammaire…

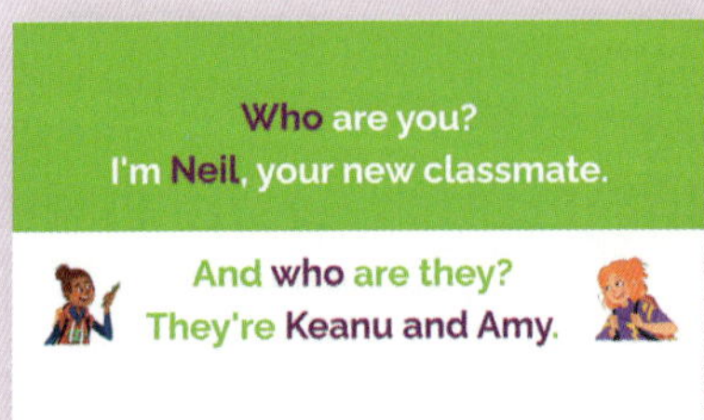

… des **tutos** pour **expliquer visuellement** les points les plus compliqués

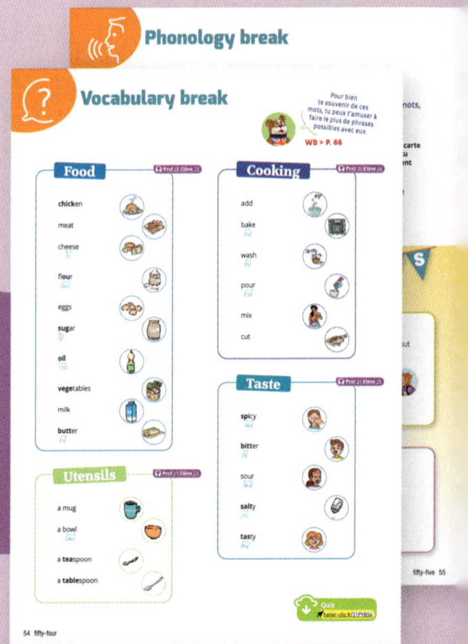

Dans les *Grammar* et *Vocabulary Breaks*…

… **27 jeux interactifs** pour te tester en **grammaire et vocabulaire**

hatier-clic.fr 21PYB1

Sur hatier-clic.fr, j'indique le code ressource du pictogramme !

Page *Time to play*...

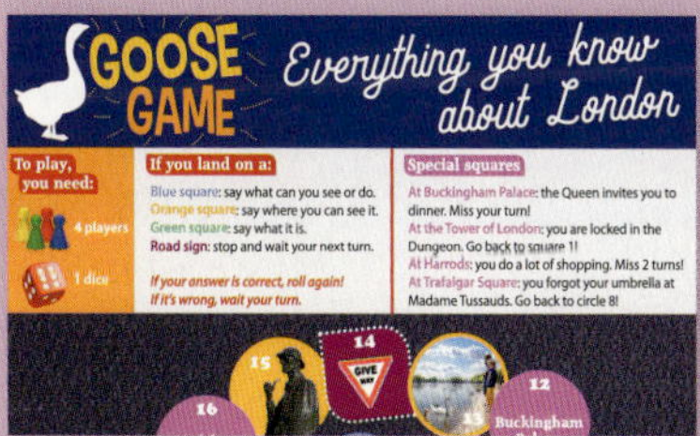

... 5 plateaux de jeux pour t'amuser en ligne avec tes camarades

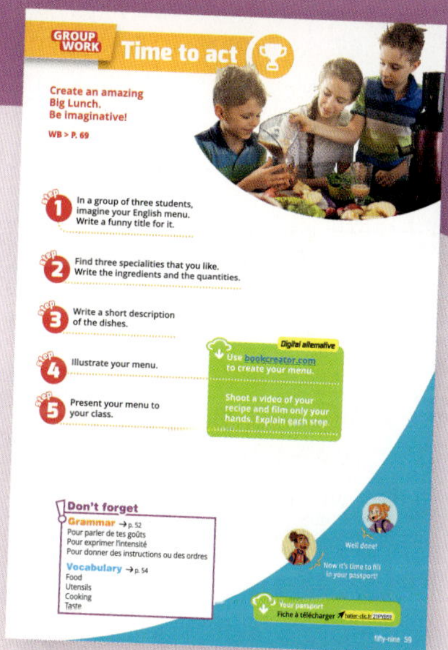

Dans *Time to act*...

... des **projets en version digitale** pour varier les formes de tes réalisations

Pour accompagner les fêtes...

... des **posters animés** pour aller à la découverte des fêtes anglosaxonnes

A treasure hunt in Hawaii

Time to act

- Play a battleship game in Hawaii.

1. Look at the three pictures.
2. Say what you can. WB > P. 9

Your goals

Dans ce voyage à Hawaii, tu vas :

- Revoir et consolider ce que tu as pu voir à l'école primaire.
- Apprendre à te présenter et à connaître tes camarades de classe.
- Découvrir le début des aventures d'Amy et Keanu.

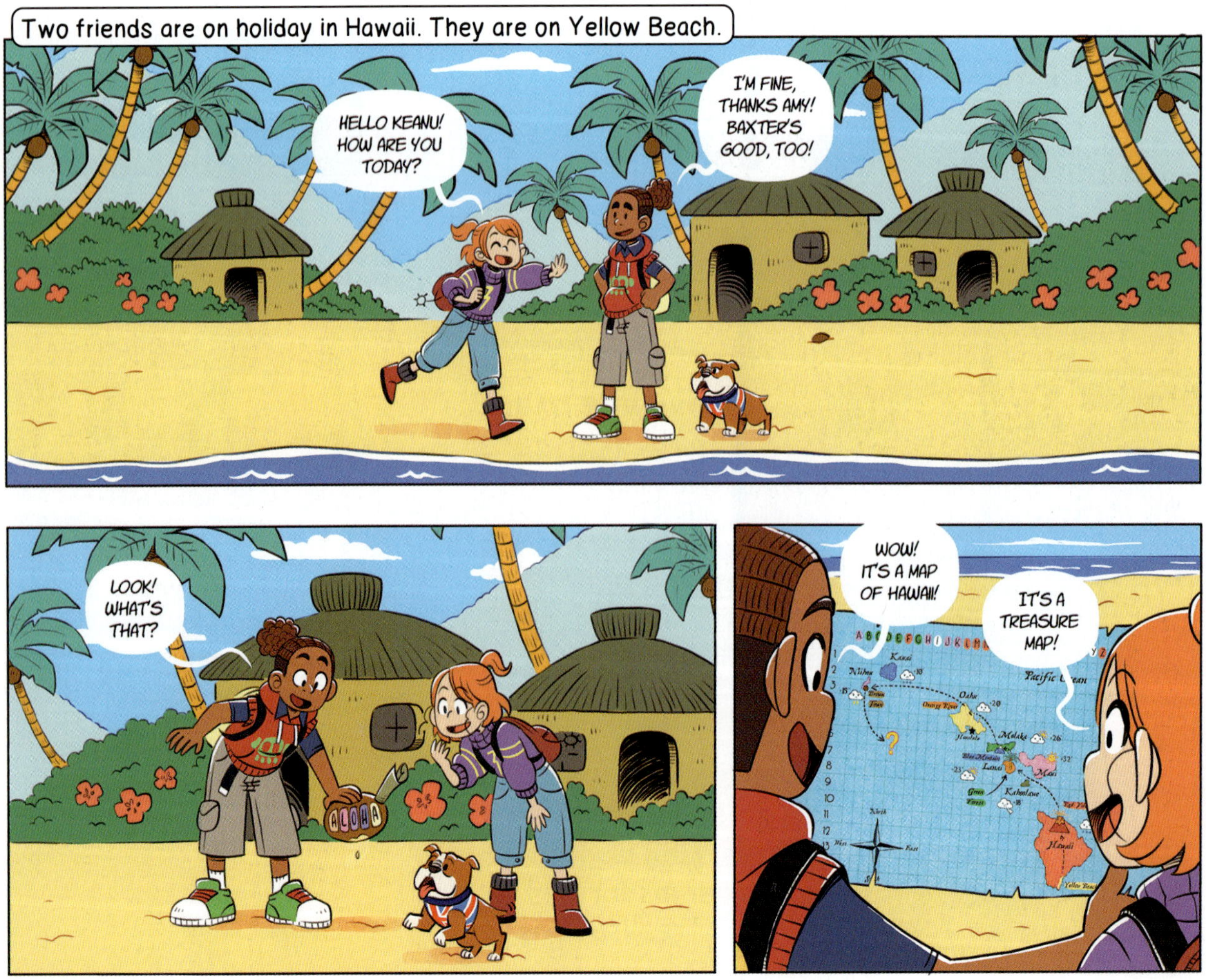

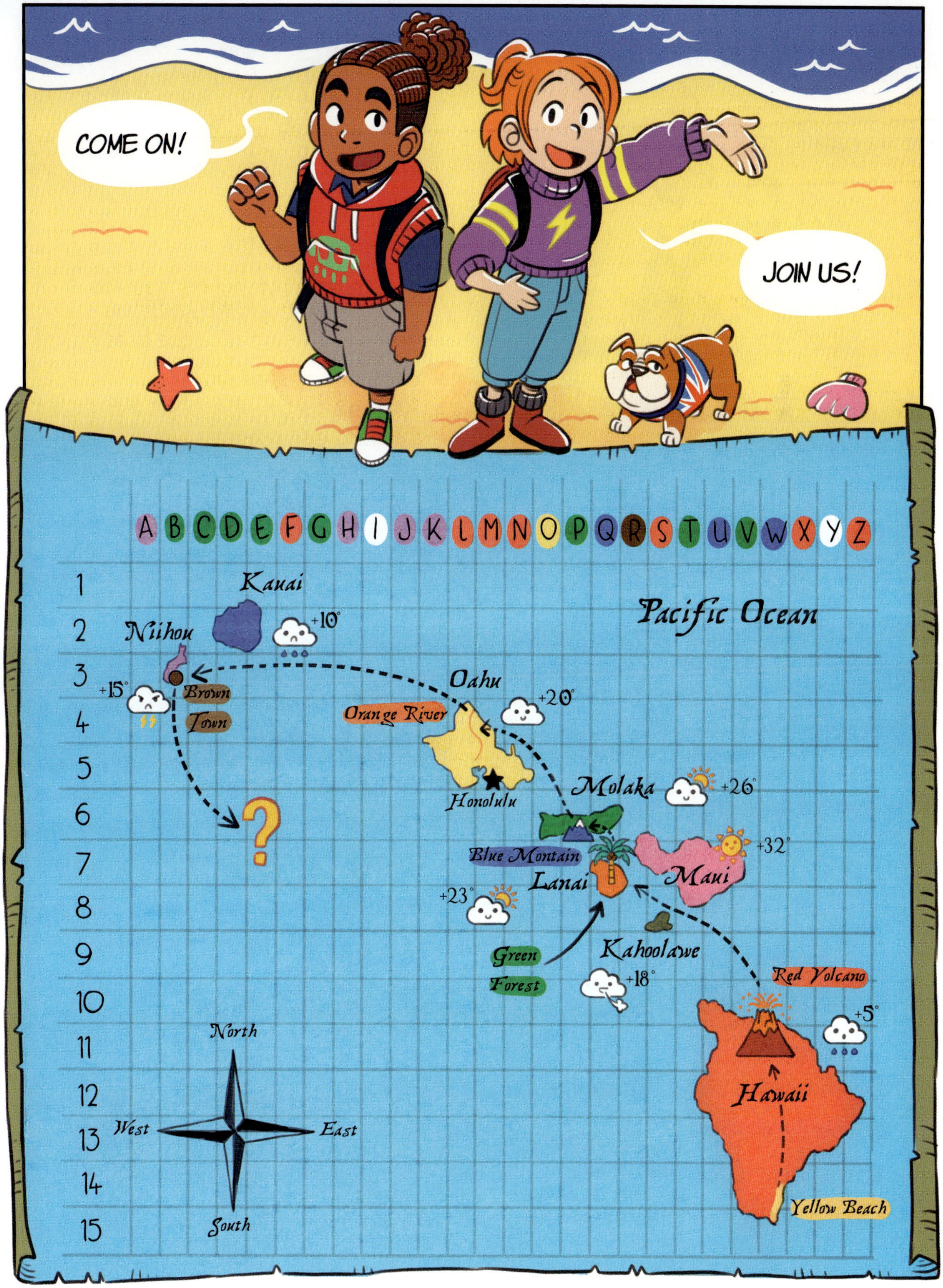
COME ON!
JOIN US!
A B C D E F G H I J K L M N O P Q R S T U V W X Y Z
1 2 3 4 5 6 7 8 9 10 11 12 13 14 15
Kauai
Niihou
+10°
Pacific Ocean
+15°
Brown Town
Oahu
Orange River
+20°
Honolulu
Molaka
+26°
Blue Montain
Lanai
Maui
+32°
+23°
Green Forest
Kahoolawe
+18°
Red Volcano
+5°
Hawaii
Yellow Beach
North
West
East
South

Puzzles

PUZZLE 1 What is your name? Video

hatier-clic.fr/21PYB14

Je suis là pour t'aider ! Pour gagner l'étape jaune, tu vas épeler ton prénom !

1. Watch the video and revise the English alphabet.
2. Use the letters of your first name to write a rap with English words you know.
3. Say your name and rap for the class. WB > P. 10

My first name is...

Now go to red puzzle!

PUZZLE 2 Let's count

Pour gagner l'étape rouge, tu vas additionner des nombres.

Hawaii in numbers

Hawaii is one state in the United States of America.
There are eight islands in Hawaii.
There are three volcanoes.
There are two official languages: Hawaiian and English.
There are twelve letters in the Hawaiian alphabet.

1. Read the text.
2. Spot the numbers.
3. Calculate the total. WB > P. 10

One state plus eight islands equals nine...

4. **PAIRWORK** Count in twos! Then in threes! And then in fives!

0-2-4...

Now go to green puzzle!

PUZZLE
3 Know your colours

Mixing Colours

'I love you, forever.'
Say the colours together.
Black, White, Red, Blue and Yellow
Have five little babies who say
'Hello!'

Pour passer l'étape verte, tu vas parler des couleurs et de leurs mélanges.

Hawaii is the Rainbow State!

Do you know the colours of the rainbow?

1. Read the poem.
2. Identify the colours in the text.
3. Look at the treasure map. **WB > P. 13** Say the colours of the islands. **WB > P. 12**
4. Say what colours the babies are.

Now go to blue puzzle!

PUZZLE
4 What is the weather today?

Sunday Monday Tuesday Wednesday Thursday Friday Saturday

1st first	2nd second	3rd third	4th fourth	5th fifth	6th sixth	7th seventh	8th eighth	9th ninth	10th tenth	11th eleventh	12th twelfth	13th thirteenth

14th fourteenth	15th fifteenth	16th sixteenth	17th seventeenth	18th eighteenth	19th nineteenth	20th twentieth	21st twenty-first	22nd twenty-second
23rd twenty-third	24th twenty-fourth	25th twenty-fifth	26th twenty-sixth	27th twenty-seventh	28th twenty-eighth	29th twenty-ninth	30th thirtieth	31st thirty-first

January February March April May June
July August September October November December

Pour passer l'étape bleue, tu vas présenter la météo du jour.

1. **GROUP WORK** Choose an island on the map, p. 13. Tell the weather. Your friends guess where you are.
2. Say a date to your friends. Your friend writes the date down. **WB > P. 13**
3. Find a classmate with a birthday in winter, in spring, in summer and in autumn.

It's hot and sunny. 32 degrees celsius.

Oh! You're in Maui!

Tips
In the United Kingdom, the temperature is in **Celsius**.
In the United States, the temperature is in **Fahrenheit**.

Go to orange puzzle!

Puzzles

Pour passer l'étape orange, tu dois dire ton nom, ton âge, d'où tu viens, ta nationalité et où tu habites.

PUZZLE 5 Two extraordinary teenagers

Audio

Tips

Countries' names and their inhabitants

The United States of America (USA) = American
England = English
Ireland = Irish
Scotland = Scottish
Wales = Welsh

1. Listen to the recording and write down the information (names, ages, countries, nationalities). Prof 1 **WB > P. 15**
2. Say what you can for each person (girl, boy, parents, grandparents). **WB > P. 16**
3. Say where you are from and where you live.

Go to brown town!

My parents are from ...

I live in ...

PUZZLE 6 The final clue

Audio

C'est l'étape finale ! Tu vas suivre des indications pour trouver le trésor caché...

Tips

Cardinal points

1. Listen to the recording and note down the indications (number of spaces, direction, the letter and number of the square). Prof 2 **WB > P. 17**
2. Follow the directions on the map.
3. Say where the treasure is and what it is.

PAIR WORK Time to act

Play battleship in Hawaii!

WB > P. 18

step 1 Hide the different elements on the islands in Hawaii. No elements in the ocean! Only on an island.

step 2 Ask your partner questions about where the different elements are.

step 3 The first person to find all the elements wins the treasure!

Is the volcano in L20?

Yes! The volcano is in L20. Is the treasure chest in F11?

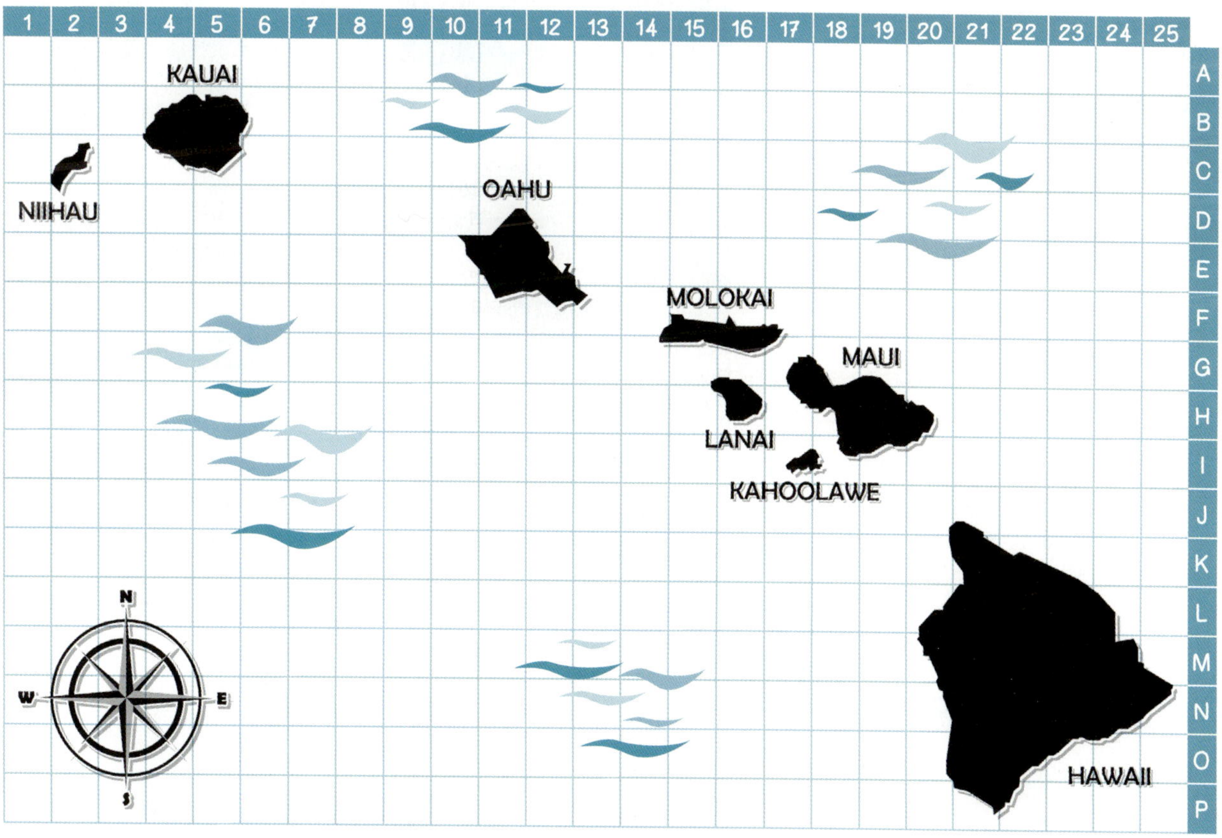

Trip 1 New school, new friends, new me

Time to act

- Present a dream school for the Dream School Contest.

Prepare your trip

Look at the photo. Describe what you see. Guess what time of year it is. **WB > P. 19**

Watch the video. Prof 1
Speak about the feelings of the pupils in their new school.
List the facilities of this school.

Visit the Project Britain website. Find out information about arrival at school. hatier-clic.fr/21PYB18

Your goals

Avec ce voyage, tu vas :

- Découvrir une école comme Poudlard.
- Parler des uniformes et du matériel scolaire.

First day at school.

Downloads EXTRA RESOURCES FOR TEACHERS

→ Tips to survive the first days at secondary school

→ How to organise your school bag

ACCESS TO YOUR *digital tools*

Quest 1 Welcome to secondary school!

A First day of school

Timetable for Kingsland Secondary School students					
	Monday	**Tuesday**	**Wednesday**	**Thursday**	**Friday**
8:30 a.m.	**Registration**				
8:35 a.m.	**Assembly**				
8:50 a.m.	Maths	History	Geography	English	Computer studies
9:40 a.m.	Science	Computer studies	English	History	English
10:30 a.m.	**Morning break**				
10:40 a.m.	Geography	French	Music	French	French
11:30 a.m.	**Lunchtime**				
12:20 p.m.	English	Art	French	Science	Maths
1:10 p.m.	PE	Maths	Maths	Science	Music
2:00 p.m.	**Afternoon break**				
2:20 p.m.	History	Drama	Science	Maths	PE
3:10 p.m.	**End of the school day**				

1. Look at the timetable for Year 7. Say what time the pupils arrive at school. **WB > P. 20**
2. List the school subjects.
3. Give the times for:
   - the first lesson,
   - the morning break,
   - lunch,
   - the last lesson.

Grammar

- Pour dire l'heure, tu dis *IT'S* :
  10:56 = *ten fifty-six*
  8:15 = *eight fifteen / a quarter past eight*
  8:45 = *eight forty-five / a quarter to nine*
  13:30 = *one thirty pm / half past one*
- Pour parler de ce que tu possèdes, tu dis *I HAVE GOT*.

Vocabulary

a break
a snack
a **pe**riod /ɪə/
a **pen**cil **shar**pener
a **rub**ber
a **ru**ler
a **note**book
a **pen**cil case
a **high**lighter /aɪ/
a **pen**cil
a pen
a **time**table /aɪ/
PE = **Phys**ical Edu**ca**tion

Prof 3 Elève 1

B What's in my school bag? Video

1. Look at the title of the activity and the picture. Say what you can.
2. Watch the video. Take notes about the school objects. **WB > P. 22**
3. Recap what you know.
4. **PAIR WORK** Say what is in your school bag!

C School uniforms Audio

1. Listen to the recording and spot the different parts of the school uniform. Prof 4
2. Name the pieces of the uniform. **WB > P. 23**
3. Listen again and check.
4. Recap the school uniform for girls and boys.

Girls wear a blouse, a tie, but not boots.

Boys wear trousers but not jeans.

Mini challenge GROUP WORK

Create a cool school uniform **WB > P. 24**

Each group picks elements for the new uniform (clothing, colours, accessories).

Draw a picture of the new uniform.

Present your uniform to the class.

Quest 2

What house are you in?

Quand tu lis un texte, repère qui parle à qui. Cela t'aidera à comprendre la situation.

D The houses of Hinchley Wood School

Audio

determined · clever · generous · courageous · patient · peaceful · creative · caring

1. Listen and learn about the house system. Prof 5
2. Match the adjectives with the correct house. **WB > P. 26**

E The Sorting Hat

"Welcome to Hogwarts," said Professor McGonagall. "Here, you are sorted into your houses. The Sorting is a very important ceremony because your house will be something like your family. You have classes with the rest of your house, sleep in your house dormitory, and spend free time in your house common room."

"The four houses are called Gryffindor, Hufflepuff, Ravenclaw, and Slytherin. Each house has its own noble history. While you are at Hogwarts, your triumphs earn your house points, while any rulebreaking loses house points.

✦ *Harry Potter and the Philosopher's Stone* by J.K. Rowling

1. Read the text. Find the names of the different houses. **WB > P. 27**
2. Say the activities pupils do with their houses.
3. Give details about the points system.

Grammar

Pour donner un ordre, tu utilises l'impératif : *Talk to the other pupils.*

Vocabulary

sleep	ad**ven**ture
dormitory /ɔː/	**hu**mour
free time	**loy**alty /ɔɪ/
classes	earn
trust	lose
re**spect** /ɪ/	

Prof 6 Elève 2

F New friends

1. Say hello and smile.

2. Start a conversation.

3. Be kind and introduce yourself.

4. Play nicely and keep in touch.

Friends are important in Year 7!

Come on and make friends with us!

1. Look at the drawings. Say what you can.
2. Read the captions. Say something for speech bubbles. **WB > P. 28**
3. **PAIR WORK** Write a new caption and illustrate it.

G Friendship soup

Video

Parcours citoyen

We are all special and unique. But it's important to understand and appreciate the similarities and differences between people. **WB > P. 29**

1. Watch the video and say what a friendship soup is. **WB > P. 28**
2. List the ingredients.
3. **GROUP WORK** Decide on four ingredients for your friendship soup.

Mini challenge GROUP WORK

Imagine a house for your school WB > P. 30

Choose a name, an adjective and characteristics. Then create a badge.

Our house is named Sherlock Holmes House.

Students are clever and determined.

Grammar break

Quiz
hatier-clic.fr/21PYB24

Pour dire l'heure

Pour demander l'heure en anglais, tu dis : *WHAT TIME IS IT?*
Pour dire l'heure, tu utilises les chiffres de 1 à 12 en ajoutant *a.m.* pour les heures avant midi et *p.m.* pour les heures après-midi. Tu fais précéder l'heure de *IT'S*.

8:10 = *It's eight ten a.m.*

15:20 = *It's three twenty p.m.*

Si l'heure est pile, tu peux utiliser l'expression *O'CLOCK*.

18:00 = *It's six o'clock. / It's six p.m.*

Pour les minutes de 1 à 30, tu peux utiliser *PAST* en indiquant les minutes avant l'heure.

18:05 = *It's five past six.*

Pour les minutes de 30 à 59, tu peux utiliser *TO* en indiquant les minutes avant l'heure.

10:50 = *It's ten to eleven.*

Il existe quelques heures particulières :

12:00 = *It's **noon**. / It's **midday**.*

00:00 = *It's **midnight**.*

14:30 = *It's **half past** two.*

9:15 = *It's **a quarter past** nine.*

9:45 = *It's **a quarter to** ten.*

Exercices

WB > P. 31

1 Donne l'heure de deux façons différentes.
Ex.: 8:30 = It's eight thirty. / It's half past eight.

a. 9:40
b. 11:15
c. 1:00
d. 12:05
e. 12:55

2 Donne l'heure pour chaque horloge.

a. 

b. 

c. 

d. 

3 Dis à quelle heure tu fais les activités suivantes un jour d'école.

a. I wake up at...
b. I eat breakfast at...
c. I arrive at school at...
d. My first lesson is at...
e. I have a break at...
f. I eat lunch at...
g. School ends at...

Pour parler de ce que tu possèdes

WB > P. 22

Pour indiquer ce que tu possèdes, tu utilises *HAVE* ou *HAVE GOT* pour toutes les personnes, sauf à la 3ème personne du singulier.

*I **have got** black shoes.* *We **have got** black trousers.*

À la forme négative, tu utilises *HAVEN'T GOT*.

*They **haven't got** their blazers.*

À la forme interrogative, tu inverses le verbe et le sujet. Tu peux répondre brièvement par *YES, I HAVE* ou *NO, I HAVEN'T*. *GOT* disparaît dans les réponses brèves.

Have you got a blue pen?

*No, I **haven't**.*

Exercices

4 Construis des phrases à l'aide des mots suivants en utilisant « *have got* » à la bonne forme.

a. I / a blue book (*affirmative*)
b. They / four pencils (*négative*)
c. We / two schoolbags (*affirmative*)
d. You / blue pens (*négative*)

5 Réponds à chaque question.

Ex.: Have you got a pencil case?
➡ Yes, I have / No, I haven't.

a. Have you got a school uniform in France?
b. Have we got a tie?
c. Have they got their timetable?
d. Have we got a break at ten o'clock?
e. Have you got activities after school?

Pour donner des ordres

WB > P. 28

Pour donner des ordres, il faut utiliser l'impératif. L'impératif se construit à partir de la base verbale.

Tuto
hatier-clic.fr/21PYB25

***Play** with the other pupils!*

À la forme négative, tu ajoutes *DON'T* devant la base verbale.

***Don't wear** jeans at school.*

Exercices

WB > P. 32

6 Remets les mots suivants dans le bon ordre.

Ex.: in / ! / eat / class / Don't
➡ Don't eat in class!

a. your / friends / homework / Do / with / .
b. have / lunch / Don't / alone / .
c. teachers / Talk / with / your / .
d. fight / Don't / with / pupils / other / .
e. leggings / wear / Don't / school / at / .

7 Donne quatre consignes aux élèves pour bien travailler à l'école. N'oublie pas d'utiliser aussi la forme négative.

Ex.: Be nice with your teachers. Don't be late for school.

8 Imagine les ordres que Dumbledore donne à ses élèves.

a. 
b. 
c. 
d. 

Vocabulary break

Tu peux facilement repérer les noms propres car ils commencent par une majuscule.

WB > P. 33

School uniform

Prof 7 Elève 3

a **jum**per 

a tie 

a **bla**zer /eɪ/ 

a shirt /ʃɜː/ 

a skirt 

trousers 

School material

Prof 9 Elève 5

a **rub**ber 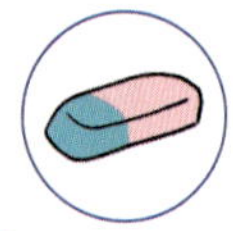

a **note**book 

a **pen**cil case 

a pen 

a **pen**cil 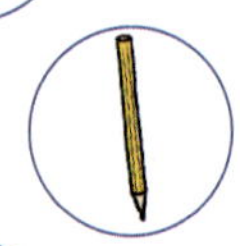

a **high**lighter 

a **pen**cil **shar**pener 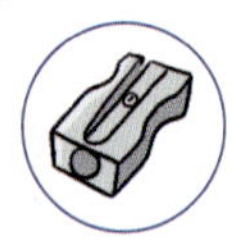

School subjects

Prof 8 Elève 4

Maths 

English 

History 

PE 

Science 

Friendship

Prof 10 Elève 6

trust /ʌ/ 

res**pect** 

humour /juː/ 

kindness /aɪ/ 

Quiz
hatier-clic.fr/21PYB26

Phonology break

Prononcer la voyelle « a »

Parfois A se prononce avec :
un son long comme pour *"star"* /stɑː/,
un son court comme pour *"cat"* /kæt/
ou une diphtongue comme pour *"name"* /neɪm/ ou *"case"* /keɪs/.
Les diphtongues sont des voyelles dont la prononciation glisse d'un son à un autre.

Exercices

Écoute ces phrases et répète-les.
Prof 11 Elève 7

a. A fat cat sat on a mat.
b. Mark is very smart.
c. I park my car in the parking lot.
d. A black hat is in the bag.
e. Five blind mice.
f. An apple a day keeps the doctor away.
g. Mike likes singing on a mike.
h. In July, I buy a kite.

WORD GAMES

Game 1

Scrambled letters

Put the letters in the right order and find the hidden word.

Ex. : Sehos = shoes

a. hghiltigher
b. culacloatr
c. srhapneer
d. rebubr

Game 2

The lost syllables

Find the lost syllable for each word.

a. bla	1. zer
b. jum	2. pect
c. trou	3. ness
d. res	4. per
e. kind	5. mour
f. hu	6. sers

Game 3

The odd one out

Find the word that does not go with the other words in the list.

Ex. : period – break – lesson – school bag.
The odd one out is "school bag"!

a. half – quarter – pupil – o'clock
b. skirt – shirt – pencil – tie
c. scissors – ruler – listen – glue
d. respect – trust – smile – fight

Time to discover

Do you walk to school?

Yes, I do! It's important to be active.

A Why is walking to school important? Look at the documents.

1 Describe the pictures (people, information, objects).

2 Find where the pictures come from.

3 Say why it is important to walk to school.

B Now be creative! Create your poster to organise a "Walk to school" day.

1 Create a poster to promote a "Walk and cycle to school" day.

2 Write three reasons why it is important to walk and cycle to school.

Get inspired!

Learn and play about your Health

Being physically active is important!

GROUP WORK

Time to play

Get ready to play BINGO!

Look at the picture. Name the elements.
You have one minute!

Now play BINGO!

Choose a bingo card. Listen to the teacher. Mark the elements on your card. Say "bingo!" when your card is complete.

Time to check

1 Vérifie tes connaissances

WB > P. 34

A. Observe et décris.

Regarde la photo ci-contre et imagine toutes les fournitures scolaires que la fille peut porter dans son sac à dos pour qu'il soit aussi lourd.

2 Fais le point sur tes compétences

WB > P. 34

B. Écoute et comprends.

Audio Prof 12 Elève 8

Écoute Kate et complète le programme d'une journée type de collège en Grande-Bretagne.

Time of the day	What pupils do

C. Écris les règles de vie de classe de ton cours d'anglais.

Fais au moins cinq phrases pour présenter les règles de vie de classe de ton cours d'anglais. Aide-toi des éléments ci-dessous.

1

2

3

4

5

6

7

3 Progresse en anglais

D. Fais ces activités en ligne pour t'entraîner et t'améliorer.

Activités de remédiation
hatier-clic.fr/21PYB30

GROUP WORK

Time to act

Present a dream school for the Dream School Contest.

WB > P. 36

step 1 Choose a name and location for your dream school.

step 2 Decide the school subjects and imagine a timetable for a typical day: arrival at school, lesson times, breaks, lunch, activities, end of school.

step 3 Give the elements of the school uniform.

step 4 Draw the school or make a model.

Digital alternative
Create your school online: https://floorplancreator.net/

step 5 Present your dream school to the class.

Don't forget

Grammar → p. 24
Pour dire l'heure
Pour parler de ce que tu possèdes
Pour donner des ordres

Vocabulary → p. 26
School uniform
School subjects
School material
Friendship

Well done!

Now it's time to fill in your passport!

Your passport
Fiche à télécharger hatier-clic.fr/21PYB31

Trip 2

Wow! I'm a superhero!

Time to act

- Create a cover for a new superhero comic book and win "The Superhero Comic Book challenge".

Prepare your trip

Look at the photo. Name the superheroes you know. **WB > P. 37**

Listen to the audio. Prof 13 Elève 9
Write the names and details of the superheroes described. **WB > P. 37**

Visit the Marvel website hatier-clic.fr/21PYB32
to find more information about superheroes.

Marvel DC Lunch atop a skyscraper, by Dan Avenell.

Your goals

Avec ce voyage, tu vas :

- Découvrir l'univers des superhéros et superhéroïnes et leurs superpouvoirs.
- Décrire tes superhéros préférés.
- Rencontrer des superhéros et superhéroïnes du quotidien.
- Présenter un superhéros ou une superhéroïne.

Downloads

EXTRA RESOURCES FOR TEACHERS

- → Let's Be Superheroes, song
- → The superpowers of superheros, song
- → Superheroes' headquarters

ACCESS TO YOUR digital tools

Quest N 1

All about superheroes

Repère les mots qui ressemblent au français. Ils t'aideront à comprendre.

A The (secret) identities of superheroes

Audio

1

2

1. Listen and identify the superheroes (name, age, job, origin, city). Prof 14 Elève 10 WB > P. 38
2. Listen and choose the picture with the correct superhero and superheroine. Prof 15 Elève 11
3. Give information about one of the following superheroes: physical appearance, costume, accessories. Your classmates guess his / her name.

Guess who has got a black costume!

I know! It's...!

Thor | Captain America | Black Widow | Okoye

Grammar

> *BE* permet d'exprimer qui tu es : identité, âge, taille, personnalité.
> *Wonder Woman **is** tall and very athletic. She **is** American.*

Vocabulary

belt	lance
mask	tall ≠ small
cape /eɪ/	round /aʊ/ ≠ square /ɛə/
gloves	straight ≠ **cur**ly
costume	dark ≠ light /aɪ/
shield /iː/	**side**kick
hammer	

Prof 16 Elève 12

B The friends and enemies of superheroes

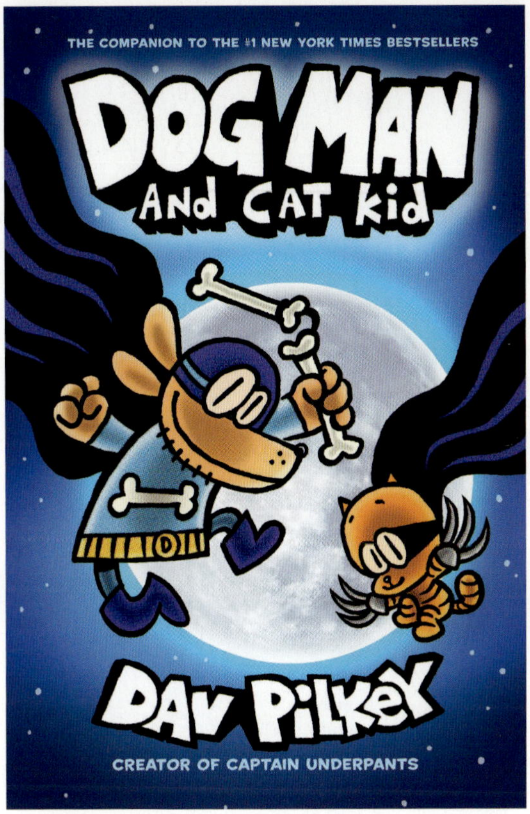

✦ *Dog Man and Cat Kid,* by Dav Pilkey, Scholastic publisher (Graphix), 2017. Front cover.

✦ Back cover.

1. Look at the front cover and the back cover. Imagine Dog Man's story.
2. Now read the text. Say who is who.
3. Describe Dog Man and Cat Kid. **WB > P. 40**
4. Read the back cover and recap what people think about Dog Man.

DOG MAN has got an interesting story. He has got the body of a man with the head of a dog! Dog Man and Cat Kid, his sidekick, are a fun duo because in real life dogs and cats don't like each other. Cat Kid is adorable and he's very smart. Dog Man is a policeman. He always fights the new bad guy in town. The story is very funny.

Mini challenge PAIR WORK

The "sidekick" challenge WB > P. 41

Imagine you are a superhero or a superheroine. Choose secretly a sidekick in your class. Your classmate asks questions to discover who it is.

Yes, my sidekick is a girl.

Has she got long hair?

Quest N 2

Everyday (super)heroes

Regarde les images avant de commencer ta lecture. Elles t'aideront à mieux comprendre le texte.

C Ordinary girls can change the world

✦ *Primer's*, by Thomas Krajewski and Jennifer Muro (art: Gretel Lusky), 2020.

Ashley is a young girl. Art is her passion. One day she finds some spray paint cans in a room. Her life changes forever. She puts this special body paint on her. Each colour gives her a different power. She can manipulate fire and ice, teleport or fly. She has practically every superpower imaginable! Now she has a secret identity: Primer. She can also fight crime. But can she save the world from dark forces?

1. Look at the first picture and read the text. Say who Primer is and what she can do. **WB > P. 42**
2. Look at the second picture and list Primer's other superpowers.

   With green paint, she can fly.

3. Test your memory about Primer's superpowers. Close your book and ask your classmates five questions.

Grammar

- Pour dire ce que tu es capable de faire, utilise *CAN* avec la base verbale, à toutes les personnes : *Primer **can** turn invisible.*
- Pour dire ce que tu ne peux pas faire, utilise *CAN'T*. *Primer **can't** climb up buildings.*

Vocabulary

fly /aɪ/
shoot
time **tra**vel /æ/
con**trol** vege**ta**tion
fight /aɪ/
shrink
save
climb up /aɪ/
teleport /ɪ/
cou**ra**geous
brave /eɪ/
ordinary **peo**ple
helpful
in**vin**cible
do good deeds
real life

Prof 17 Elève 13

D We can all be (super)heroes

Parcours citoyen

1. Describe this poster and say what you understand. **WB > P. 44**
2. Read and say what makes an everyday superhero.
3. Give examples of everyday superheroes.

E How to be a real-life superhero

Audio

1. Listen to the audio and list the different tips to be a superhero. Prof 18 **WB > P. 45**
2. Say how else you can help others.

Mini challenge

'Be a superhero' posters WB > P. 45

Your school is organising a "Be a superhero" festival.

Make a class poster with all the actions you can do to be an everyday superhero or superheroine. Don't forget to illustrate your actions and write a title.

Grammar break

Quiz
hatier-clic.fr/21PYB38

Pour présenter une personne

WB > P. 40

Pour présenter une personne, tu utilises *BE* :

- l'identité : *She **is** Wonder Woman.*
- l'âge : *She **is** 24 (years old).*
- l'origine : *She **is** from the USA.*
- la nationalité : *She **isn't** British.*
- la description physique : *She **is** athletic.*
- la personnalité : *She **is** courageous.*

À la forme interrogative, on inverse le sujet et *BE*. *BE* se place en première position.

__Is__ she American?

À l'oral, à la forme affirmative et négative, on utilise souvent la forme contractée de *BE*. La première lettre est remplacée par une apostrophe.

*He **is** tall. ➡ He**'s** tall.*

Dans les réponses courtes, on ne peut pas contracter les verbes.

__Is__ Dog Man a policeman? *Yes, he **is**.*

Pour parler de ce qu'une personne possède, tu utilises *HAS GOT* à la troisième personne du singulier.

	BE	*HAVE GOT*
Forme affirmative	*She **is**... / She**'s**...*	*He has got... / He's got...*
Forme négative	*She **is** not... / She **isn't**...*	*He has not got... / He hasn't got...*
Forme interrogative	***Is** she...?*	*Has he got... ?*
Réponse courte	*Yes, she **is**. / No, she **isn't**.*	*Yes, he has. / No, he hasn't.*

Exercices

WB > P. 46

1 Complète les phrases avec *BE* conjugué à la forme affirmative ou négative.

a. Superman ... Peter Clarke.
b. He ... small.
c. He ... 45.
d. Superman ... from Metropolis.
e. Dog Man ... a cat.
f. Cat Kid ... a sidekick.

2 Regarde ces objets et fais des phrases pour dire si les superhéros suivants les possèdent ou pas.

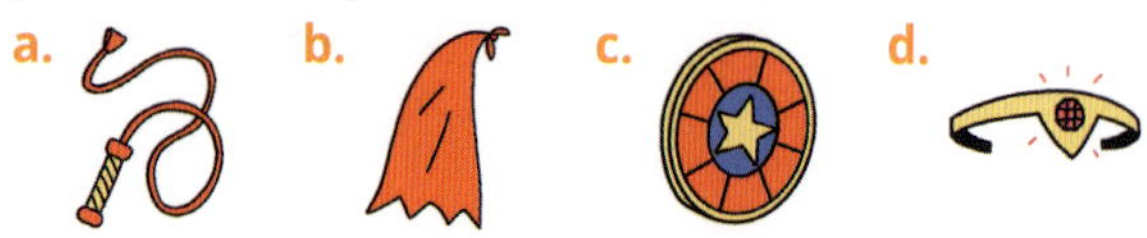

Wonder Woman – Captain America – Thor – Okoye

3 Pose des questions à ton ou ta camarade concernant les objets de l'exercice 2.

Ex.: Has Okoye got a cape?

Pour exprimer la possession WB > P. 39

**Pour indiquer ce qu'une personne possède, tu utilises les déterminants possessifs.
Si le possesseur est masculin, on dit *HIS*. Si le possesseur est féminin, on dit *HER*.
Le déterminant possessif peut être suivi d'un nom singulier ou pluriel.**

Pronoms personnels sujets	*He*	*She*
Déterminants possessifs	*His*	*Her*

***His** boots are black.*

***Her** boots are black.*

Exercices

WB > P. 46

4 Remplace les taches d'encre par le déterminant possessif qui convient.

a. Wonder Woman has a cape: … cape is red.
b. … name is Cat Kid.
c. For Primer, art is … passion.
d. Dog Man is a superhero. Cat Kid is … sidekick.

Pour parler de ce que tu sais faire WB > P. 43

Pour parler de ce que tu es capable de faire, tu utilises *CAN*.

*Superman **can** fly.*

Pour parler de ce que tu es incapable de faire, tu utilises *CAN'T* ou *CANNOT*.

*Superman **can't** climb up buildings.*

***CAN* est invariable ; il est toujours suivi de la base verbale.
À la forme interrogative, *CAN* se place avant le sujet.**

Can Primer fly? Yes, she can.

Tuto
hatier-clic.fr/21PYB39

Exercices

WB > P. 46

5 Remets les mots dans le bon ordre.

a. shoot / can't / She / lasers / .
b. Primer / manipulate / can / fire / .
c. you / Can / parks / clean up / ?
d. fly / Dog Man / can / bad guys / fight / but / can't / he / .

6 Écris des phrases pour parler des capacités de ce superhéros.

a.

b.

c.

d.

e.

f.

Vocabulary break

Dans ton workbook, légende les dessins avec le vocabulaire appris.

WB > P. 48

Physical description

Prof 19 Elève 14

straight hair /ɛə/

curly hair

round face /aʊ/ /eɪ/

square face /ɛə/

small nose

big nose

brown eyes /aɪ/

tall

Clothes and accessories

Prof 20 Elève 15

costume

suit /uːt/

gloves /ʌ/

glasses /ɪz/
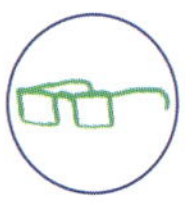

shield

hammer

Powers

Prof 21 Elève 16

fly

ma**nip**ulate fire /eɪ/

paint

climb up **build**ings /aɪ/
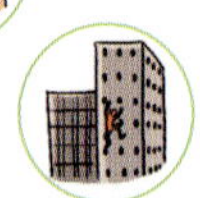

fight crime

turn in**vis**ible

save the world /eɪ/

grow **su**per giant-size /eɪ/

shrink **su**per small

Quiz
hatier-clic.fr/21PYB40

Phonology break

La voyelle « i »

En anglais, le « i » peut se prononcer de deux manières différentes. Il peut être court comme dans « big » /ˈbɪg/ ou long comme dans « shield » /ʃiːld/.

Ex.: Cat Kid is an athletic policeman.
/ɪ/ /ɪ/ /iː/

Observe ces deux phrases :

Look at the sheep! /iː/ *Look at the ship!* /ɪ/

En fonction de ta prononciation, on ne comprendra pas la même chose à l'oral.

Exercices

1 Écoute, répète et entraîne-toi.
Prof 22 Elève 17

magazine – is – electronic – machine – policeman – different – interesting – athletic – piece – give – team

« Can » et « Can't »

La voyelle « a » dans *CAN* et *CAN'T* ne se prononce pas de la même manière.

- Pour les questions et les réponses brèves, *CAN* est accentué et on le prononce /ˈkæn/.

Ex.: Can Primer fly? Yes, she can.

- Pour les affirmations, *CAN* se prononce /kən/ et il n'est pas accentué.

Ex.: Primer can manipulate fire and ice.

- Pour les négations, *CAN'T* se prononce toujours /ˈkɑːnt/. Il est toujours accentué.

Ex.: Cat Kid can't turn invisible.

Exercices

2 PAIR WORK Pose des questions à ton camarade sur ce qu'il sait ou ne sait pas faire. Attention à la prononciation !

Pupil A: Can you run very fast?

Pupil B: Of course I can!

WORD GAMES

Game 1

The vocabulary supergenius

Look at the picture on pages 32-33.

Say a word to describe an element in the picture. The next person repeats the word and adds a new one. If it's not a new word, you lose.

Game 2

Dress my superhero

Imagine the costume of a new superhero.

Describe the different elements to your partner. He / She can draw it.

Time to discover

Look! Street art can represent superheroes too!

✦ *Game Changer,* by Banksy.
He is a street artist. He represents problems of everyday society in his art.

✦ *Hero II,* by Ben Turnbull, 2010.
Ben Turnbull's "Supermen – An Exhibition of Heroes" features patriotic images like the faces of firemen.

A Describe the two pictures.

1 In picture one, imagine why the little boy prefers playing with the superheroine nurse.

2 In picture two, say why this man can be a superhero.

B Now you're the artist! Create a class poster composed of all the everyday heroes you can think of.

1 **GROUP WORK** Each group decides which superhero / superheroine they want to represent (people you know or famous people).

2 Draw him or her (or find a picture).

3 Give details about this person in a few words (name, qualities, "superpowers"…).

4 Add a catchy slogan to convince your classmates to act.

5 Cut your work out and paste it on the class poster.

Get inspired!

- Banksy: Who is the famous graffiti artist?
- Banksy pays superhero tribute to Britain's NHS staff

PAIR WORK

Time to play

Secret Superhero Game

Ask for clues to find out which superhero the other player thinks of.

Plateau de jeu
hatier-clic.fr/21PYB43

Time to check

1 Vérifie tes connaissances

WB > P. 49

A. Observe et décris.

Regarde l'illustration ci-dessous et fais un maximum de phrases commençant par :
He / she has got...
He / she is...

2 Fais le point sur tes compétences

WB > P. 49

B. Lis et comprends.

Lis le texte et essaie de retenir un maximum d'informations sur ce superhéros.

Livre fermé, décris ce superhéros à ton ou ta camarade.

Ton ou ta camarade doit te dire si tes phrases sont exactes.

My name is Superguy, I am 28 years old. I am tall and very strong. I have got a blue and red costume. I have got yellow gloves and dark blue boots. My shield is round and flashy. I have got short straight blond hair and blue eyes. I can climb up high buildings and I can teleport, but I can't shoot lasers. I am the new superhero. I can save the world!

3 Progresse en anglais

C. Fais ces activités en ligne pour t'entraîner et t'améliorer.

Activités de remédiation
hatier-clic.fr 21PYB44

Time to act

Create a cover for a new superhero comic and win the "The Superhero Comic Book challenge"!

WB > P. 51

step 1 Imagine a superhero or a superheroine. Write a short description of his / her physical appearance and his / her costume.

step 2 Write a short description of your superpowers.

step 3 Write the description of his / her sidekick, his / her enemy and other elements of your choice.

step 4 Place these elements on the back cover.

step 5 Create the book cover:

- draw a picture,
- write a title for your comic book,
- write your magic sentence in a bubble.

Digital alternative

Create your digital book cover and back cover. You can use the app Book Creator: https://bookcreator.com/

step 6 Present your cover and back cover to the class. Be convincing!

Don't forget

Grammar → p. 38
Pour présenter une personne
Pour exprimer la possession
Pour parler de ce que tu sais faire

Vocabulary → p. 40
Physical description
Clothes and accessories
Powers

Well done!

Now it's time to fill in your passport!

Your passport
Fiche à télécharger hatier-clic.fr/21PYB45

Trip 3 The amazing world of food!

Time to act

- Make an amazing menu for your school Big Lunch.

Prepare your trip

Look at the map and say what the countries have in common. WB > P. 52

Visit the Commonwealth's website for kids. hatier-clic.fr/21PYB46

Listen to the recording and say what the food speciality is. Prof 23 Elève 18

Your goals

Avec ce voyage, tu vas :

- Découvrir de nouveaux plats et aliments.
- Pouvoir dire ce que tu aimes et ce que tu n'aimes pas.
- Suivre et donner des indications pour réaliser un dessert.

Every year, people from the Commonwealth have a Big Lunch together.

Downloads

EXTRA RESOURCES FOR TEACHERS

- → English food
- → Organise a Big Lunch
- → The Duke and Duchess of Cambridge prepare a Big Lunch

ACCESS TO YOUR *digital tools*

Quest N 1

Finger-licking good

Quand tu écoutes un enregistrement pour la première fois, repère les mots porteurs de sens, ici, les ingrédients.

A British food

Audio

1

2

3

1. Listen to the recording and say the names of the British food specialities. Prof 24 Elève 19
2. Name as many ingredients as you can. **WB > P. 53**
3. Say what speciality you like.

Grammar

Pour dire ce que tu aimes ou n'aimes pas, tu utilises les verbes de goût :
*I **like** vegetables.*
*I **hate** mushrooms!*

Vocabulary

salty /ɔː/
sweet
creamy /iː/
juicy /uː/
tasty /eɪ/
crunchy /ʌ/
crispy /ɪ/
bitter
chewy
spicy /aɪ/

Prof 25 Elève 20

B Australian snacks

Video

Tips

Vegemite is an Australian food.
It is salty and bitter.

1. Say what the situation is. **WB > P. 54**
2. Watch the video. Identify the ingredients.
3. Say if the kids like the snacks or not.

The boy likes...
The girl doesn't like...

C Salt and pepper or chalk and cheese?

1. Choose three food items you like.
2. **PAIR WORK** Ask your classmate questions about the food he / she likes. **WB > P. 56**
3. Say if you are "salt and pepper" or "chalk and cheese".

Mini challenge

Favourite foods! WB > P. 57

Choose your favourite dish and list the ingredients.
Draw it.
Tell the class why you like it.

I like... because...

I prefer... because...

What food do you like?

I like spicy food. I like curry!

Quest 2 Yummy cakes!

Pour anticiper l'écoute, regarde les visuels.

D Delicious desserts

Audio

ANZAC BISCUITS

150g flour
100g oats
80g [illegible]
165g sugar
150g butter
4 tbsp [illegible]

CLASSIC ENGLISH TRIFLE

750g red [illegible]
250g sugar
1 litre custard
1,2 litre milk
400 ml [illegible]
2 sponge cakes

HUMMINGBIRD CAKE

370g flour
1/2 tsp salt
4 [illegible]
225g [illegible]
3 eggs
160ml oil
200g sugar

1. Look at the pictures and say what you can.
2. Listen to the recording and find the missing ingredients.
   Prof 26 WB > P. 58
3. **GROUP WORK** Play a card game. Match the ingredients to the correct dessert. You have two minutes!

Tips

teaspoon (tsp)	gramme (g)	millilitre (ml)
tablespoon (tbsp)	litre (l)	kilogramme (kg)

Grammar

> Pour expliquer une recette, utilise l'impératif :
Crack the eggs.

Vocabulary

flour /aʊ/	cake /eɪ/
eggs	whisk
milk	crack
sugar	add
cream /iː/	bake /eɪ/
biscuits /ɪ/ /ɪ/	**sep**arate /ɛ/
pudding /ʊ/	whip

Prof 27 Elève 21

E Let's get cooking!

Video

Prof 4

Concentre-toi sur les mots que tu connais.

1. Look at the photo. Say what you think it is.
2. Watch the video and name the ingredients you recognise. **WB > P. 59**
3. Give your opinion about pavlova.

F Sugar substitutes

Parcours santé

Honey

Maple syrup

Dates

Many people think white sugar is an essential ingredient in their kitchen. But there are healthy substitutes.

1. Say what sugar alternative you prefer.
2. Rewrite the recipe for Anzac biscuits using a sugar alternative. **WB > P. 61**
3. Name the other ingredients you can change.

Mini challenge

The dessert recipe challenge! WB > P. 62

Choose your favourite dessert.
Write down the ingredients and the quantities.
Write down five steps and illustrate them.

The class votes for its favourite dessert recipe.

I like your recipe because it looks...

I prefer Paul's dessert because...

Grammar break

Quiz
hatier-clic.fr/21PYB52a

Pour parler de tes goûts

WB > P. 60

Pour parler de tes goûts, tu utilises *LOVE*, *LIKE*, *ENJOY*, *DON'T LIKE*, *HATE* au présent simple. Après ces verbes, il peut y avoir un groupe nominal ou un verbe.

I **hate** *onions.*
sujet + verbe de goût + groupe nominal

I **enjoy** *eating pancakes.*
sujet + verbe de goût + base verbale + *-ing*

Le verbe *PREFER* signifie qu'entre plusieurs choses, il y en a une qu'on aime plus.

I **prefer** *desserts.*

Tuto
hatier-clic.fr/21PYB52b

Exercices

WB > P. 63

1 Remets les mots dans le bon ordre.
À l'écrit, pense à commencer tes phrases par une majuscule.

Ex.: not / they / do / like / peppers / .
➡ They do not like peppers

a. pancakes / love / I / .
b. not / they / eggs / do / like / .
c. you / Indian / do / like / food / ?
d. does / eating / Juliet / dislike / meat / ?
e. food / not / spicy / eating / he / does / like / .

2 Remplace les icônes par le verbe de goût correspondant.

Ex.: She 🤢 ... fish .
➡ She hates fish / eating fish.

a. I 😍 ... sausages.
b. She 🤢 ... broccoli.
c. Do they 🙂 ... cooking pasta?
d. You 🙁 ... English breakfast.
e. Jack 😐 ... trying new foods.

3 Keanu t'a écrit un SMS dans lequel il te dit ce qu'il aime et n'aime pas. Écris quelques phrases pour parler de ses goûts.

a. 😍 / 🍫 ...
b. 🙂 / 🍦 ...
c. 🙁 / 🌶️🥕🍅 ...
d. 🤢 / 🐟 ...

Pour exprimer l'intensité

WB > P. 56

Pour exprimer l'intensité, tu utilises des adverbes de degré.
Ils se placent toujours devant le verbe, l'adjectif ou l'adverbe qu'ils modifient.

*I **really** hate garlic.* *I **quite** like chicken.* *I don't like chicken **at all**!*
*I **rather** love curry.*

Exercices

WB > P. 64

4 Complète les phrases avec les bons adverbes de degré.
a. Zoe likes fruit for breakfast.
b. I like fish and chips.
c. They like dessert.
d. Does Charlie love pavlova?
e. I like cooking.

5 Remets les mots dans le bon ordre.
a. love / really / I / pavlova / .
b. rather / we / food / spicy / like / .
c. Jules / red / hates / really / fruits / .
d. Alison and Luke / not / do / like / really / meat and fish / .

6 Écris quelques phrases pour exprimer les goûts d'Amy en utilisant des adverbes de degré.
a. 😍 / strawberries
b. 🙂 / Vegemite
c. 😕 / vegetables

Pour donner des instructions ou des ordres

WB > P. 61

Pour expliquer une recette, tu utilises l'impératif.
L'impératif se construit uniquement avec la base verbale.

***Cut** strawberries. **Bake** for 25 minutes.*

À la forme négative, tu ajoutes *DON'T* devant la base verbale.

***Don't add** too much sugar!*

Exercices

WB > P. 65

7 Utilise les éléments suivants pour donner des instructions pour réaliser des pancakes.

Verbs	Ingredients	Utensils
add	flour	bowl
crack	sugar	wooden spoon
whisk	baking powder	pan
mix	milk	
pour	eggs	
serve	butter	
put	whipped cream	

8 Retrouve les quatre instructions données par l'infirmière du collège pour une alimentation saine.
water / don't buy / eat / food / too much / vegetables / drink / fruit / don't eat / and / sugar / industrial

Vocabulary break

Pour bien te souvenir de ces mots, tu peux t'amuser à faire le plus de phrases possibles avec eux.

WB > P. 66

Food

Prof 28 Elève 22

chicken 

meat 

cheese /iː/ 

fl**our** /aʊ/ 

eggs 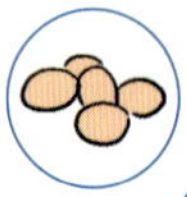

sugar /ʃ/ 

oil /ɔɪl/ 

vegetables 

milk 

butter /ʌ/ 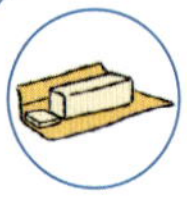

Utensils

Prof 29 Elève 23

a mug 

a bowl /əʊ/ 

a **tea**spoon 

a **table**spoon 

Cooking

Prof 30 Elève 24

add 

bake /eɪ/ 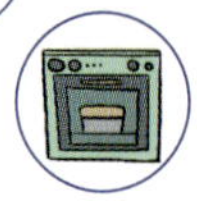

wash /ɒ/ 

pour /ɔː/ 

mix 

cut 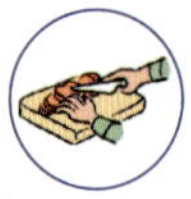

Taste

Prof 31 Elève 25

spicy /aɪ/ 

bitter /ɪ/ 

sour /aʊ/ 

salty /ɔː/ 

tasty /eɪ/ 

Quiz
hatier-clic.fr/21PYB54

Phonology break

Exprimer tes émotions

Pour exprimer tes émotions, tu accentues certains mots. En accentuant ces mots, tu transmets un message et des sentiments.

*Ex. : This **definitely** doesn't **taste** like a **burger**!*

Exercices

1 Écoute puis repère les syllabes accentuées. Ensuite, répète la phrase. Prof 32 Elève 26

a. I don't like it. It's not tasty at all.

b. Wow, I'm really impressed by your pancake recipe.

c. This chocolate cake is absolutely disgusting!

d. That's quite cool, good idea!

2 Pioche une carte « aliment » et une carte « émotion ». Mime ta réaction quand tu manges l'aliment. Tes camarades doivent dire si tu aimes ou pas.

Pupil A: hate – spaghetti

Other pupils: He REALLY hates spaghetti!

WORD GAMES

Game 1

Our shopping list

You want to make an apple pie. Make a list before shopping.

Pupil A: We need ...

Pupil B: We need ... and...

Pupil A: We need ..., ... and ...

Game 2

What's on my plate?

Pupil A chooses a food and describes it without giving its name.

Pupil B tries to guess the food.

It's yellow. It's sour. It looks delicious but isn't.

Is it a lemon?

Game 3

Culinary equations

Look at the ingredients and find out what dish they make.

Ex. : egg whites + sugar? = meringues

a. butter + eggs + flour + sugar = ?

b. bacon + beans + eggs + sausages = ?

c. chicken + tomatoes + curry + rice = ?

d. fish + mashed peas + chips = ?

Game 4

Find the odd one out!

Ex. : milk – maple syrup – flour – oil
Flour! It's not a liquid!

a. bacon – chicken – apples – sausages

b. flour – sugar – vanilla extract – onions

c. trifle – pavlova – fish and chips – cake

d. cheese - coconut - yoghurt - cream

Time to discover

That's my breakfast! It's not art!

Yes, it is. Food can be art.

✦ *Portrait of Taylor Swift*, by Sarah Rosado.
She is an artist from New York City. She makes art with breakfast cereals. She makes amazing portraits of celebrities.

✦ *Wotsit all about*, by James Ostrer.
He is a British photographer. He uses junk food in his art.

A Look at the artworks.

1. Say what they are made of.
2. Give examples of junk food.
3. Say which piece of art you prefer.

B Create food art!

1. Choose the ingredients.
2. Make your artwork.
3. Take a picture of your creation.
4. Show your artwork to your friends.

Get inspired!

- Crazy Food Art
- This fashion illustrator makes masterpiece sketches out of food, plants and more

GROUP WORK

Time to play

Read the titles.
Find the missing words in the text.
Match the texts with the correct photos.

a

b

c

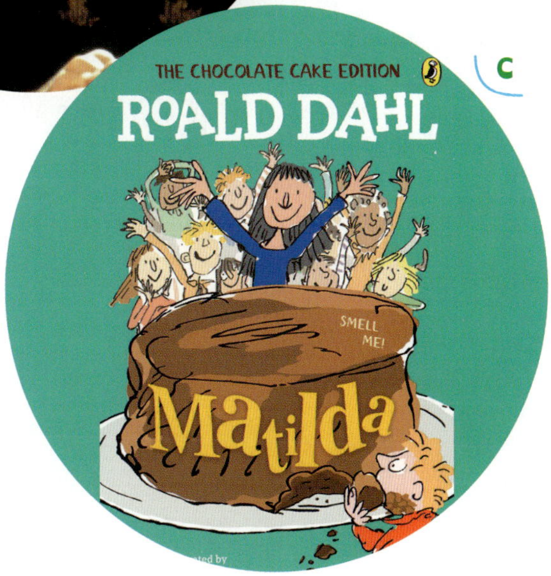

1

Bogtrotter's chocolate ...

Bogtrotter likes your cake. He adores your cake. (...) The cook was back again staggering under the weight of an enormous round chocolate cake on a china platter. The cake was covered with dark-brown chocolate icing.

✦ *Matilda*, Roald Dahl

2

Large ... cakes

Harry opened the last present to find a new, hand-knitted sweater from Mrs Weasley and a large plum cake.

✦ *Harry Potter and the Chamber of Secrets*, J. K. Rowling

3

Bilbo Baggins's extra ... cakes

"My good sir," said Balin with the white beard. "I don't mind some cake-seed-cake, if you have any."

✦ *The Hobbit*, J.R.R. Tolkien

Time to check

1 Vérifie tes connaissances

WB > P. 67

A. Observe et décris.

Regarde l'illustration et écris la liste de tous les ustensiles et aliments que tu vois.

2 Fais le point sur tes compétences

WB > P. 67

B. Écoute et comprends. Audio — Prof 33 Elève 27

Sally va manger chez John.
Écoute leur conversation et liste les ingrédients pour le dîner.

C. Écris une recette.

Écris au moins cinq phrases pour rédiger la recette du Sticky Toffee Pudding en t'aidant de la liste des ingrédients et des illustrations.

3 Progresse en anglais

D. Fais ces activités en ligne pour t'entraîner et t'améliorer.

Activités de remédiation
hatier-clic.fr/21PYB58

GROUP WORK

Time to act

Create an amazing Big Lunch. Be imaginative!

WB > P. 69

step 1 In a group of three students, imagine your English menu. Write a funny title for it.

step 2 Find three specialities that you like. Write the ingredients and the quantities.

step 3 Write a short description of the dishes.

step 4 Illustrate your menu.

step 5 Present your menu to your class.

Digital alternative

Use bookcreator.com to create your menu.

Shoot a video of your recipe and film only your hands. Explain each step.

Don't forget

Grammar → p. 52
Pour parler de tes goûts
Pour exprimer l'intensité
Pour donner des instructions ou des ordres

Vocabulary → p. 54
Food
Utensils
Cooking
Taste

Well done!

Now it's time to fill in your passport!

Your passport
Fiche à télécharger hatier-clic.fr/21PYB59

Trip 4 Awesome British families!

Four generations of royals together for Christmas.

Time to act

- Make "Did you know?" cards to have fun with your friends.

Prepare your trip

Look at the photo. Describe what you see. WB > P. 70

Watch the video. Prof 5
Learn family relations' names. Repeat them.

Visit the official Royal Family website. Find out information about its members. hatier-clic.fr/21PYB60

Your goals

Avec ce voyage, tu vas :

- Parler des liens entre les membres d'une famille.
- Décrire ce qui caractérise chacun d'eux.
- Découvrir des familles britanniques célèbres.

Downloads

EXTRA RESOURCES FOR TEACHERS

→ Who is Prince George?

→ Lindsey: I come from a large family

ACCESS TO YOUR digital tools

Quest N 1

The British Royal Family

A Royal Family but normal people

Parcours PEAC

CambridgeSussexFan + Follow

Wishing a very happy birthday to Charles, Prince of Wales! 🎉 🎊

I love this photo! Everybody looks so happy! It's nice to see Prince Charles with his wife, his two sons and his grandchildren reunited! Kate and William's children look happy. George is funny and his sister Charlotte is cute next to Camilla. Louis is just adorable! Harry and Meghan look great too! Grandpa Charles is lucky to celebrate his birthday with his beautiful family! 🎂 😍 💖

3542 likes

1. Read this Instagram post.
2. Say who these people are. **WB > P. 71**
3. Give details about their relationships.
4. Say which event they celebrate.

Grammar

Pour parler des relations entre les membres d'une famille, utilise **le génitif**. Pour cela, tu ajoutes *'S* à la fin du nom.

*He is **William's brother**.*

*They are **Charles's sons**.*

Vocabulary

a **grand**father /ð/	a wife /aɪ/
a **grand**mother	a **hus**band /ʌ/
grand**chil**dren /tʃ/	a child, **chil**dren
a **fa**ther	a **broth**er
a **moth**er	a **sis**ter
a **step**father	a son
a **step**mother	a **daugh**ter /ɔ/

Prof 34 Elève 28

B A princess at school

Audio

1. Listen to the dialogue between Charlotte and Suzy. It's their first day at school. Prof 35
2. Look at Charlotte's family tree. Who are her parents? And her grandparents? **WB > P. 73**
3. Say who can become queen or king in this family.

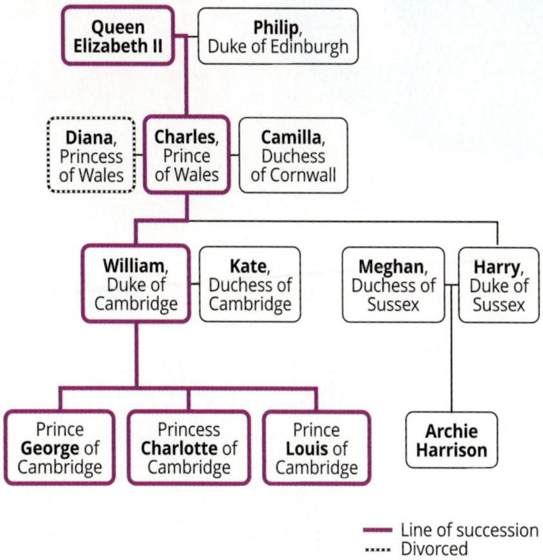

C The Queen is a pet lover

Audio

1. Listen to an enthusiastic fan. Prof 36
2. Say who she is a fan of.
3. Give details on the Queen's passion.
4. Are other members of the Royal Family pet lovers too? Give examples. **WB > P. 74**

D The Queen and her beloved corgis

1. Describe this film poster.
2. Show why this photo is funny.
3. Imagine what the dog thinks: write a caption.

Tips

On the throne, the British Queen wears a crown, a royal cape and a sceptre.

Mini challenge

PAIR WORK

Guess who **WB > P. 74**

Pupil A: Choose one member of the Royal Family. Create a riddle (*devinette*) with at least four elements. Use the genitive for one element.

Pupil B: Guess who this person is.

Then swap roles.

She is a girl. She is the Queen's great-granddaughter...

She is Charlotte!

Quest N 2

A family full of mysteries

Sur l'affiche d'un film, les photos et le texte te donnent des indices pour imaginer l'histoire.

E The girl in red

✦ *Enola Holmes,* movie directed by Harry Bradbeer.

1. Look at the document and describe it. **WB > P. 76**
2. Describe the girl. Who is she?

I think this girl is... because...

I can see... I think..

Grammar

- Pour exprimer une similitude avec une autre personne, tu peux utiliser *like* devant un nom.
  *She's **like** her mother.*
- Ou alors tu peux utiliser *too* en fin de phrase.
  *She's curious **too**.*

Vocabulary

in**tell**igent	ad**ven**turous /tʃə/
joyful /dʒ/	brave /eɪ/
curious	ener**get**ic /dʒɛ/
strict	**play**ful
serious /ˈsɪəriəs/	
dy**nam**ic /aɪ/	

Prof 37 Elève 29

F Mystery runs in the family

Video

1. Watch the video. Draw Enola's family tree.
2. Say why Eudoria is not an ordinary mother. WB > P. 78
3. Say what you know about Enola's brothers. Who is her favourite brother? Give details.
4. Describe Enola's personality. Is she different from the other members of her family?

alone ≠ together

I think Enola looks funny!

Yes! She is funny! Like her mother!

Mini challenge

You and your family WB > P. 79

Compare yourself to your family.

Choose members of your family. Say what you have in common with them (personality and / or interests).

My brother is cute, I'm cute too!

I'm curious like my father.

Grammar break

Quiz
hatier-clic.fr/21PYB66a

Pour indiquer la parenté, la possession

WB > P. 80

Tu utilises le **génitif** (aussi appelé **cas possessif**) pour indiquer un lien de parenté ou pour dire qui est le possesseur d'un objet ou d'un animal. Tu ajoutes *'S* entre les deux mots.

⚠ L'ordre des mots est inversé en anglais par rapport au français. C'est le possesseur qui vient en premier.

They're the Queen's great-grandchildren.

It's the Queen's hat.

Après un nom au pluriel, tu ajoutes seulement l'apostrophe.

They are my brothers' pets.

Si le pluriel ne prend pas de *S*, tu dois ajouter *'S* pour former le **génitif**.

Look at his children's grandparents!

Tuto
hatier-clic.fr/21PYB66b

Exercices

WB > P. 80

1 Remets les mots dans le bon ordre.

Ex.: Charlotte / Louis / George / sister / and / 's / is / .
➡ Charlotte is Louis and George's sister.

a. Archie / Harry and Meghan / son / 's / is / .
b. Harry / Camilla / William / is / 's / stepmother / and / .
c. great-grandmother / is / Elizabeth II / Charlotte / 's / .
d. Meghan / Harry / wife / is / 's / .

2 Utilise le génitif et les éléments ci-dessous pour faire des phrases complètes.

Ex.: Camilla / William and Harry (stepmother) / .
➡ Camilla is Harry and William's stepmother.

a. Charlotte / Louis and George (sister) / .
b. Meghan / Charlotte (aunt) / .
c. Elizabeth II / Charlotte, Louis and George (great-grandmother) / .
d. William / Kate (husband) / .
e. Harry / George (uncle) / .
f. Louis / Harry (nephew) / .

Pour poser une question sur la quantité

WB > P. 81

Pour poser une question sur une quantité avec un nom dénombrable (que tu peux compter : 1, 2, 3, etc.), tu utilises *HOW MANY* + un nom pluriel.

*"**How many** brothers has Enola got?" "She has got **two** brothers."*

Exercices

WB > P. 81

3 Remets les mots dans le bon ordre.

Ex.: they / many / have / got / How / cousins / ?

➡ How many cousins have they got?

a. Charlotte / How / has / got / brothers / many / ?
b. many / he / pets / got / has / How / ?
c. corgis / many / The Queen / got / How / has / ?
d. nieces / got / Harry and Meghan / many / have / How / ?

4 Retrouve la question qui a été posée. Utilise *How many* à chaque fois.

Ex.: They have got three children.

➡ How many children have they got?

a. She has got twelve dogs.
b. He has got one brother and one sister.
c. They have got one daughter.
d. She has got hundreds of hats.

Pour bien utiliser les articles

N'utilise pas d'article devant :

- **les titres royaux suivis d'un nom propre.**
  Tu dis : ***The** Queen* mais *Queen Elizabeth II* (pas d'article).

- **les groupes nominaux au génitif lorsqu'il commence par un prénom.**
  Tu dis : *William's brother* (pas d'article). Mais en français, tu dis : **LE** frère de William.

Exercices

5 Rajoute un article si besoin.

Ex.: Charlotte's mother is ... Duchess of Cambridge

*➡ Charlotte's mother is **the** Duchess of Cambridge.*

a. Do you know ... Prince Charles?
b. I love ... Queen!
c. ... Queen Elizabeth II wears colourful hats!
d. ... Prince Harry is ... Duke of Sussex.

Vocabulary break

Montre que tu comprends les relations entre les membres d'une famille en complétant un arbre généalogique.

WB > P. 82

Family members

Prof 38 Elève 30

a **fam**ily tree 

great-grandparents 

grandparents 

parents 

children 

mother, **fa**ther 

son, **daugh**ter 

brother, **sis**ter 

husband, wife 

Describe a personality

Prof 40 Elève 32

in**tell**igent 

joyful 

curious 

kind 

dy**nam**ic 

ad**ven**turous 

brave 

ener**get**ic 

playful 

The Royal Family

Prof 39 Elève 31

Queen, King 

Prince, **Prin**cess 

Quiz
hatier-clic.fr/21PYB68

Phonology break

Pour garder un bon rythme de phrase et donner du sens, attention de ne pas séparer les mots du groupe nominal contenant le génitif.

Prononcer le 'S du génitif.

Le *'S* du génitif peut se prononcer de trois façons différentes : /z/, /s/ ou /iz/.

Ex.: Camilla is William and Harry's stepmother.
/z/

Exercices

1 Écoute et répète chaque phrase. Note si le *'S* du génitif se prononce /z/, /s/ ou /iz/. Prof 41 Elève 33

a. William is Kate**'s** husband.
b. Charlotte is Charles**'s** granddaughter.
c. Charlotte is George**'s** sister.
d. Kate is William**'s** wife.

2 Écoute et décide du sens de *'S* : contraction de *is* ? de *has* ? ou marque du génitif ? Prof 42 Elève 34

3 Reformule chaque phrase en modifiant *'S* lorsque c'est possible. Écoute la correction et répète ces phrases. Prof 43 Elève 35

a. Charlotte's two brothers, she's the middle child.
b. Meghan's Harry's wife.
c. Archie's father's Harry.
d. "Where's Queen Elizabeth?" "She's with her husband's cousin."

WORD GAMES

Game 1
Scrambled letters

Put the letters in the right order and find the hidden word.

Ex.: dgretnamorh ➡ grandmother

a. ybab
b. istres
c. berrtho
d. adeghrtu
e. fiwe

Game 2
Family couples

Find the associated pair.

Ex.: grandmother grandfather

a. brother	1. stepmother
b. daughter	2. wife
c. uncle	3. aunt
d. husband	4. son
e. stepfather	5. sister

Game 3
Find the odd one out!

Ex.: grandmother / mother / brother / sister
➡ brother (Because it's a boy.)

a. joyful / energetic / sad / playful
b. King / Prince / Duchess / Duke
c. sister / brother / sibling / father
d. adventurous / brave / strict / curious

Game 4
Mimes

Mime an adjective of personality for your classmates.

Ex.: I think she is funny!

Time to discover

When music is a family business!

✦ Five brothers, five amazing voices!

✦ So happy with Solange and Jay Z!

A Look at the pictures.

1 Can you recognise these famous artists and their family?

2 Say who the little boy is (first photo).

3 Say who the woman in the middle is (second photo).

B Discover one of their songs.

4 The Jacksons Five: *A B C.* hatier-clic.fr/21PYB70a

5 Beyoncé: *Single Ladies* hatier-clic.fr/21PYB70b

C Listen to *We Are Family* by the American band Sister Sledge and sing along.

hatier-clic.fr/21PYB70c

D Now you're the artist! Like Sister Sledge, write a mini song about your family.

1 Choose the family members you want to talk about.

2 Give details about these people in a few words (name, qualities, hobbies...).

3 Try to be funny and convincing.

Get inspired!

Carpool Karaoke: *The Cyrus Family*

The Corrs, a hugely popular Irish band.

GROUP WORK

Time to play

Families and literature

You also know very famous families in books and films.

1. Match the book covers, the family names and a member of the family in pictures.
2. Find the names of other families in books or cartoons.

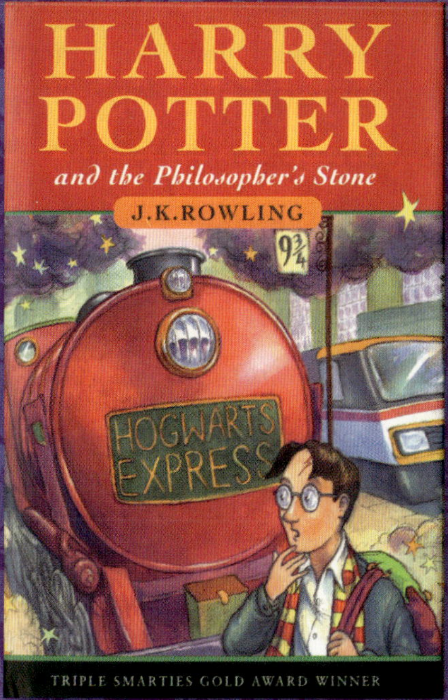

Charlie Bucket

The Weasleys

Ginny Weasley

The Buckets

Time to check

1 Vérifie tes connaissances

WB > P. 83

A. Parle de la famille royale britannique.

Ton meilleur ami doit faire un exposé en anglais sur les membres de la famille royale mais il ne les connaît absolument pas et la photo qu'il doit commenter est bien floue !

Aide-le ! Montre-lui que tu les connais bien et explique leur place dans la famille ! Donne-lui le maximum de renseignements pour qu'il réussisse son travail.

2 Fais le point sur tes compétences

B. Écoute et comprends.

Audio

Prof 44 Elève 36

Meg et son frère Ryan découvrent le quiz de la semaine dans leur magazine préféré. Meg veut répondre aux questions. Écoute ses réponses. Dis quels sont les différents aspects de sa personnalité.

C. Écris un court texte.

Écris cinq phrases au minimum pour décrire la personnalité d'un de tes amis. Lorsque c'est possible, essaie de donner des détails.

3 Progresse en anglais

D. Fais ces activités en ligne pour t'entraîner et t'améliorer.

Activités de remédiation
hatier-clic.fr/21PYB72

GROUP WORK

Time to act

Show what you know about famous families! Make "Did you know?" cards to have fun with your friends.

WB > P. 85

step 1 In groups, choose at least five interesting pieces of information about famous families. Write them on a piece of rough paper.

step 2 Read them to your teacher and decide if you keep them.

step 3 Start writing your cards.

On the **front**, write "Did you know?"

On the back of the card, write your information.

Illustrate your card with a picture or a drawing.

Digital alternative

Create a file or a slide show to present your cards. Download them on your school website.

step 4 Read your work to the class.

Don't forget

Grammar → p. 66

Pour indiquer la parenté, la possession
Pour poser une question sur la quantité
Pour bien utiliser les articles

Vocabulary → p. 68

Family members
The Royal Family
Describe a personality

Well done!

Now it's time to fill in your passport!

Your passport
Fiche à télécharger hatier-clic.fr/21PYB73

Trip 5 It's the perfect house

Time to act

- Design the rooms of your ideal house and present them to the class.

Prepare your trip

Look at the photo. Describe what you see. Guess why there are so many people. **WB > P. 86**

Watch the video. Prof 6
List all the places you visit. Say what room you prefer. **WB > P. 87**

Visit the Skateboard house website. hatier-clic.fr/21PYB74
Say what your favourite picture is.

Your goals

Avec ce voyage, tu vas :

- Découvrir des maisons américaines typiques.
- Comprendre la description d'une maison et de ses pièces.
- Parler de ce que tu fais au quotidien.

This house is similar to the house in the Pixar animated comedy, *Up*.

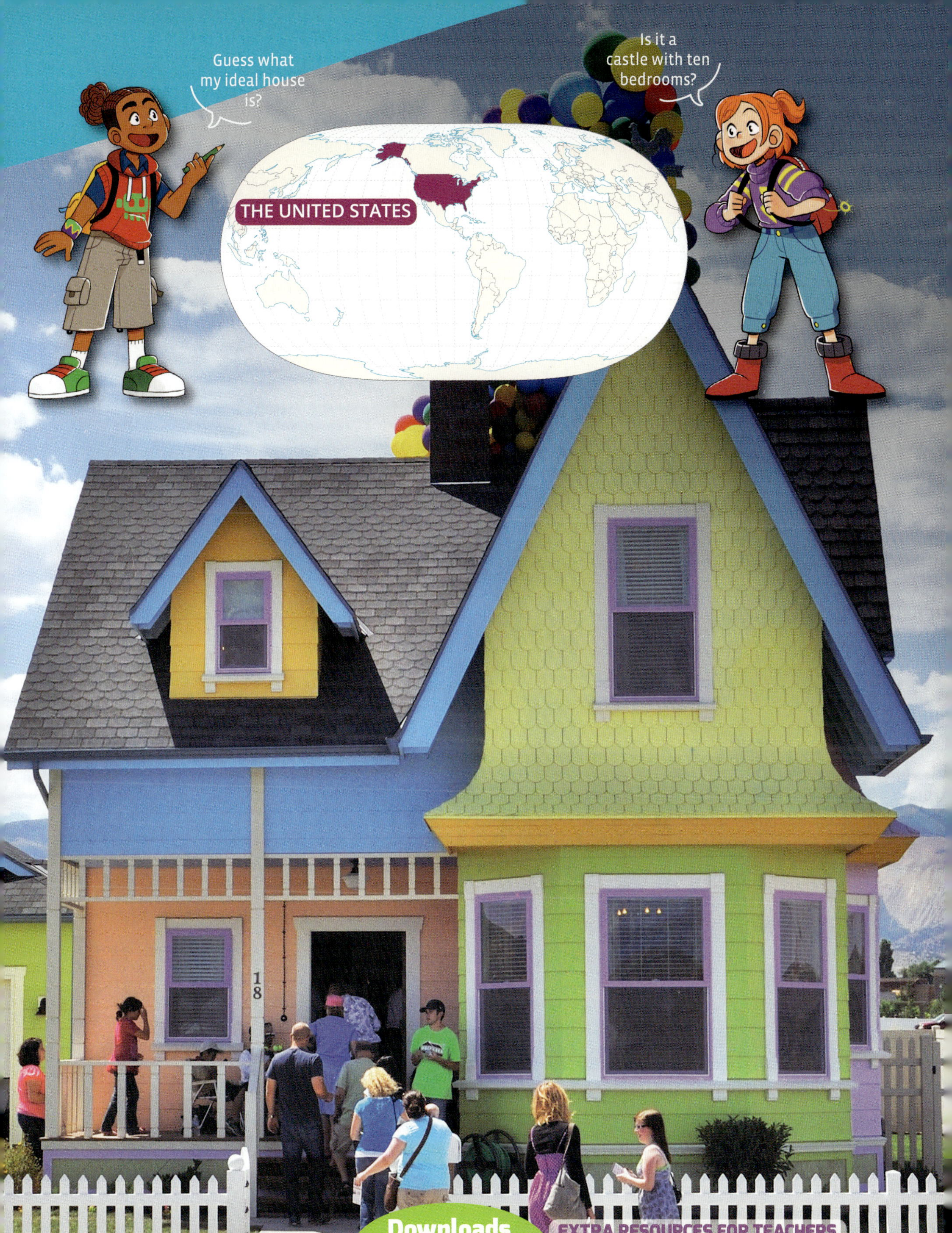

Downloads

EXTRA RESOURCES FOR TEACHERS

- → A family lives in many tiny houses
- → Hiro's family home
- → Barbie's extraordinary dreamhouse
- → Wild West filmmaking

ACCESS TO YOUR *digital tools*

Quest 1 Discover American Houses

N'hésite pas à t'exprimer en classe. Plus tu t'entraînes, plus tu progresses !

A The right House for a new movie

✦ *Beetlejuice*, movie directed by Tim Burton.

Tim Burton, a famous film director, wants to make a new Beetlejuice movie!

Come on! Help him find the perfect house!

1. Look at the movie poster.
2. Say what you can about the poster.
3. Identify the following elements: a house / a door / a roof / a window / a porch / a garden / an alley / an attic.

Number 1 is the porch.

4. Choose three adjectives in the list to describe the house: comfortable / scary / romantic / friendly / mysterious / sad / funny / big / beautiful / strange.

Grammar

Pour parler de l'endroit où se trouve une personne ou un objet, tu utilises des prépositions de lieu.
*Amy is **in** her bedroom.*
*Keanu is **behind** the house.*

Vocabulary

- an a**part**ment
- a house /aʊ/
- a de**tach**ed house /ɪ/ /æ/
- a **se**mi-de**tach**ed house
- up**stairs** ≠ down**stairs** /aʊ/
- floor /ɔː/
- a door /ɔː/
- a roof /uː/
- a **win**dow /əʊ/
- a porch /tʃ/
- a **gar**den
- an **al**ley
- an **at**tic
- a **gar**age (UK) /æ/
- a ga**rage** (US) /ə/

Prof 45 Elève 37

B Find the perfect House!

Home type: detached house
Bedrooms: 4 **Garage:** 1
Bathrooms: 2 **Attic:** 1
Location: Queens, New York

Home type: semi-detached house
Bedrooms: 4 **Garage:** 0
Bathrooms: 2 **Attic:** 1
Location: Brooklyn, New York

Home type: apartment
Bedrooms: 2 **Garage:** 0
Bathrooms: 1 **Attic:** 0
Location: Tribeca, Manhattan, New York

1. Listen to this audio. List what Tim Burton looks for. Prof 46 **WB > P. 88**
2. Look at the pictures and read their description. Say where the houses are located.
3. Say which house corresponds to Tim Burton's description. Give details to justify.

C What's inside the house?

In this film, two tiny creatures play tricks on the inhabitants.

Charles and Delia: parents
Lydia: daughter
Brad: son
Jimmy: a tiny creature
Cindy: a tiny creature

- *Charles is in the kitchen on the first floor, above the laundry room, on the right.*
- *[illegible] is in the study, next to the attic, below the roof.*
- *Lydia is in her bedroom on the [illegible] floor, on the right.*
- *[illegible] is opposite her husband. She's in the living room on the first floor.*
- *Cindy is in the garage. It's under the [illegible].*
- *[illegible] is on the stairs.*

On the first floor, there are...

1. Read Tim Burton's memo.
2. There is coffee on some of the words! Recap where the rooms are in the house. Then say which rooms the characters are in. **WB > P. 89**

Mini challenge

My extraordinary house WB > P. 90

Imagine an extraordinary house. Send a message to a friend to describe it.

Ex.:

14:52

My house looks like a shoe. There are 8 amazing bedrooms, a large garden but a tiny kitchen. There's a swimming pool in the living room.

Welcome to the Loud House!

Pour comprendre une vidéo, concentre-toi sur un type de mots. Par exemple, essaie de repérer les noms des pièces de la maison.

D Ready for the Loud House tour? Video

1. Look at the picture. Say what it is.
2. Watch the video. Note down the different rooms and the corresponding pieces of furniture. **WB > P. 91**
3. Say what you can see in Lincoln's bedroom.
4. Say what the Louds do in each room.

E Discover a room in the Loud House

1. Say what room it is. Guess what the Louds do in the evening.
2. Look at the words and choose what furniture you can see.

There is...

fridge couch bed lamp cushion bath TV coffee table

3. Describe your favourite place at home. Your friends must guess which room it is.

Grammar

- Pour parler de ce que tu fais au quotidien, tu utilises le présent simple.
  I watch TV.
  *Lincoln **combs** his hair.*
- Tu peux aussi utiliser des adverbes de fréquence, pour préciser quand tu agis.
  *I **rarely** have a bath.*

Vocabulary

a **liv**ing-room
a **bed**room
a **bath**room /æθ/
furniture /ɜ/
a couch /tʃ/
a bed

wake up /eɪ/
get dressed
shower /aʊə/
watch TV
play
go to bed

always /eɪ/
often
sometimes /aɪ/
never

Prof 47 Elève 38

F Lincoln's routine

Parcours santé

Lincoln speaking to Leni:
Everyday, I wake up at 6:30 and I get up at 7:00 a.m. I always have my breakfast very quickly in the kitchen. I often eat a burrito with extra cheese. Twenty minutes later I go to the bathroom upstairs to comb my hair and brush my teeth... err... sometimes... Then I get dressed. At 8:00 I jump into the van and I go to school.

Leni speaking to you:
Everyday he wears the same orange polo shirt. He sometimes goes to the bathroom but he is very quick to shower... yuck! He is the last one to leave the house. We always tell him to hurry up. And he is the first to go back home and do his homework. He has a snack at 5:00 p.m. and dinner at 6:30 p.m. But he never goes to bed very early. Lincoln is often tired in the morning!

1. Read the texts. **WB > P. 92**
2. Speak about Lincoln's daily routine at home.

On schooldays, go to bed early. As a preteen, you need to sleep 8 to 10 hours each night. Sleeping helps you to be healthy and concentrate at school! Don't use your smartphone or your tablet an hour before going to bed.
WB > P. 93

Mini challenge

Break the code! WB > P. 94

Make five sentences about your routine.

In one of your sentences, change one word with another word. That word starts with the same letter but it's completely different and funny.

Then read your sentences to the rest of the class.

They must guess the real word.

I brush my teeth in the bed.

...in the bathroom!

Grammar break

Quiz
hatier-clic.fr/21PYB80a

Pour indiquer la position

WB > P. 89

Pour indiquer la position d'une personne ou d'un objet, tu peux accompagner le nom d'une préposition de lieu.
Le plus souvent, ces prépositions viennent devant un nom ou un groupe nominal.
Elles sont toujours invariables, comme en français.

*Lana's pet is **on** her bed.*

*Lola is **between** Lucy and Lily.*

a.

b.

c.

d.

e.
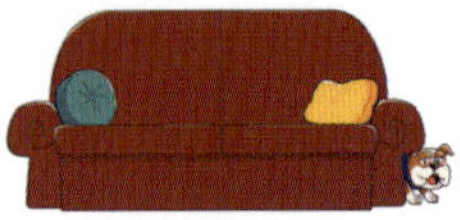

f.

g.

h.

i.

a. *in the bed*
b. *on the table*
c. *under the table*
d. *in front of the TV*
e. *behind the couch*
f. *between the chair and the lamp*
g. *next to / near the stairs*
h. *below the tree*
i. *above the baby*

Tuto
hatier-clic.fr/21PYB80b

Exercices

WB > P. 95

1 Écoute les phrases. Montre à quel dessin ci-dessus chacune correspond. Prof 48 Elève 39
*Ex.: Si tu entends **in**, montre le dessin où le chien est **dans** le lit.*

2 Imagine que le petit bulldog est quelque part dans le dessin de la chambre ci-contre. Ton ou ta camarade doit deviner où il se trouve en te posant un maximum de quatre questions. Échangez ensuite les rôles.
Ex.: "Is the bulldog on the carpet?"
"No, it isn't."
"Is the bulldog under the bed?"
"Yes, it is."

3 Observe cette chambre et lis les mots ci-dessous. Indique où les objets se situent les uns par rapport aux autres.
Ex.: football / dresser
➡ The football is on the dresser.

a. toy / box
b. magazine / bed
c. bag / pizza / chair
d. lamp / pillow
e. shoes / mirror
f. dragon / desk

Pour parler de ta routine WB > P. 93

Pour parler de tes habitudes, tu utilises le présent simple.

- Avec *I / We / You / They*, ce temps se forme avec la base verbale (sans *TO*).

  *They **sleep** in their beds.* *We **watch** TV.* *I **comb** my hair.*

- Avec *He / She / It*, il faut ajouter un *–S* à la base verbale.

  *Keanu **eats** a burrito.*

⚠ Pour certains verbes, comme *GO* ou *WATCH*, on ajoute *-ES* à la base verbale, avec He / She / It !

*Luan **watches** TV.*

Pour préciser à quelle fréquence tu fais ces actions, tu emploies un adverbe, comme *ALWAYS, OFTEN, SOMETIMES* ou *NEVER*. Cet adverbe se place devant le verbe.

*I **sometimes play** football.* *Leni **often combs** her hair.*

⚠ Avec le verbe *BE*, cet adverbe se positionne après le verbe !

*Lincoln **is never** late at school.*

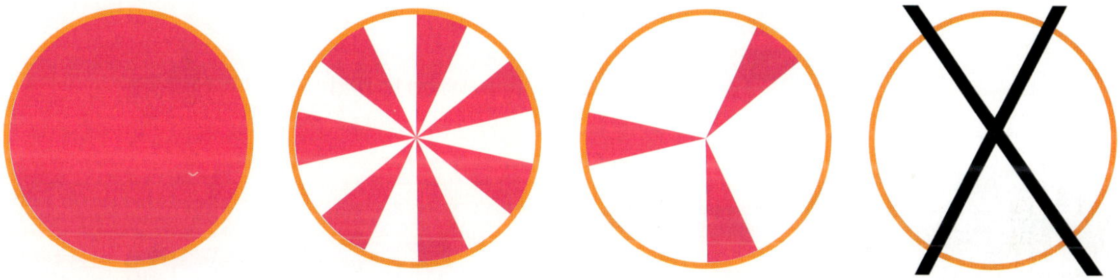

always *often* *sometimes* *never*

Exercices

WB > P. 96

4 Remplace les taches d'encre par le verbe qui convient.

Ex.: They [redacted] pizza.
*➡ They **eat** pizza.*

a. Lincoln [redacted] the same polo shirt every day.
b. Lola and Lisa [redacted] their teeth.
c. You [redacted] to bed.
d. Lincoln's Dad [redacted] his hair.
e. We [redacted] on the console.
f. Lana [redacted] a shower in the morning.

5 Place l'adverbe au bon endroit dans la phrase.

Ex.: We go to bed early. (never)
➡ We never go to bed early.

a. Lincoln jumps into the van. (always)
b. They are very silent. (sometimes)
c. Lucy goes upstairs. (often)
d. Mum is in the kitchen. (never)
e. Luna does her homework. (always)
f. We have a snack after school. (often)

6 Formule des phrases sur tes habitudes à partir des images ci-dessous. Utilise l'adverbe de fréquence qui te correspond le mieux.

Ex.:  *I always brush my teeth.*

a. 

b. 

c. 

d. 

Vocabulary break

Pour te souvenir des mots de la maison, tu peux faire des Post-it que tu colles un peu partout chez toi !

WB > P. 97

Places in the house

Prof 49 Elève 40

a **di**ning-room /aɪ/ 

a **liv**ing-room 

a **bed**room 

a **bath**room /θ/ 

a **kitch**en /tʃ/ 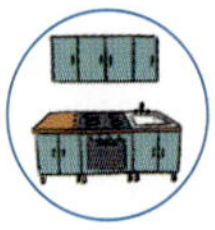

Objects in the house

Prof 50 Elève 41

a couch 

an **arm**chair 

a TV 

a desk 

a fridge 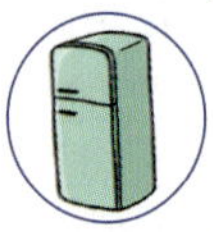

a **coff**ee **ta**ble 

a **book**shelf 

Daily routine

Prof 51 Elève 42

get up **ear**ly 

have a shower 

get dressed 

have a snack 

do my **home**work 

go to bed 

Frequency

Prof 52 Elève 43

always 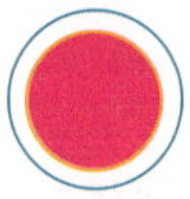

often 

sometimes 

rarely 

never 

Quiz
hatier-clic.fr/21PYB82

Phonology break

Bien prononcer les diphtongues

En anglais, on parle de diphtongues lorsque le son est composé de deux sons voyelles qui se suivent. On en prononce une et on glisse rapidement vers la seconde. Les diphtongues sont très importantes en anglais. Il faut donc apprendre à bien les prononcer !

/aɪ/ = white / sometimes *[/eɪ/ = grey / stay]* */aʊ/ = brown / couch*

À présent, entraîne-toi à répéter cette phrase le plus vite possible :

Lincoln sometimes stays near the couch.
/aɪ/ /eɪ/ /ɪə/ /aʊ/

Exercices

1 Écoute et trouve l'intrus : c'est le mot qui n'a pas la même diphtongue que les autres. Prof 53 Elève 44

Ex.: table / day / ~~night~~ / stay

a. late / eight / say / house
b. behind / hair / chair / wear
c. voice / boy / window / toy
d. go / home / no / shower
e. my / couch / night / nice

2 Écoute et repère les diphtongues. Ensuite, répète la phrase. Prof 54 Elève 45

a. The tiny creature plays in the dining room.
b. Lincoln is the only boy in this house.
c. They download movies on the computer.
d. Lori and Lana always go to bed late.
e. Luna plays music on the stairs.

WORD GAMES

Game 1

The vocabulary genius

Pupil A names an object.

Pupil B says where it is.

Ex.: "A couch?" "In the living room."
"A fridge?" "In the kitchen."

Game 2

Test your memory

Speak about Lincoln's routine in 30 seconds. Say as much as you can to win.

Ex.: Everyday, Lincoln gets up at 7.00.

Game 3

The vocabulary SUPERgenius

GROUP WORK Look at the picture of the bedroom in Grammar break, p. 80.

Say a word to describe an element of the picture. The next person repeats the word and adds a new one. If it's not a new word, you lose.

Ex.: In the bedroom, there is a bed, a computer...

Time to discover

✦ Carson Ellis is a famous illustrator. In her album, Home can be a house in the country, an apartment in the city, or ... a shoe!

A Houses fit your personality.

1 Look at the cover of Carson Ellis' book. Say what your favourite house is.
2 Describe it to your classmates who must guess which it is.
3 Look at the back cover. Say why it is strange.

B Now you're the artist!

1 Imagine and draw your wonderful house.
2 Like Carson Ellis, write a presentation of your house.

Get inspired!

@ A house in an animated comedy

@ Discover The Magic Tree House series

GROUP WORK

Time to play

It's your turn.
Throw the dice.

Upstairs! Downstairs!

To play, you need:

4 players

1 dice

Rules:

1. You must throw the dice and answer the question or describe the picture.
2. If you answer correctly, then you can move ahead one space.
3. If you don't answer a question, you miss a turn.
4. Two or more players can be on the same space.

Start

The room where you sleep is a ...?

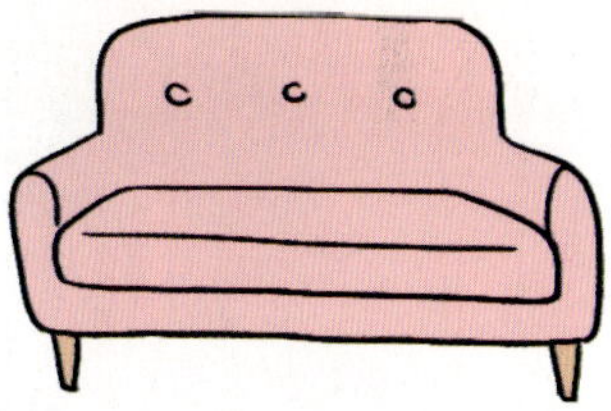

Mention three types of housing.

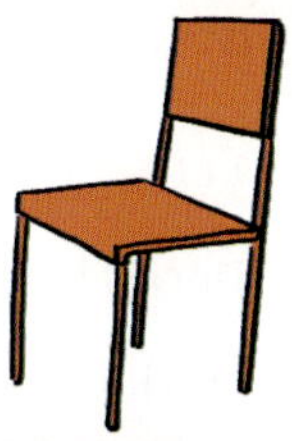

The room where you have a shower is a ...?

Finish

Plateau de jeu
hatier-clic.fr/21PYB85

Time to check

1 Vérifie tes connaissances

WB > P. 98

A. Observe et décris.

Regarde ce plan et prépare la visite de la maison.

Fais autant de phrases que tu peux, en parlant des pièces et où elles se trouvent. Donne aussi des détails sur l'ameublement.

2 Fais le point sur tes compétences

B. Écoute et comprends.

Audio

Prof 55 Elève 46

Écoute l'enregistrement.

Note les différents endroits mentionnés par Katie. Précise leur nombre.

Indique quelles sont ses pièces préférées.

BONUS : Si tu le peux, précise pourquoi ce sont ses pièces préférées.

C. Écris un court texte.

Décris les différentes routines de ta journée et celles de la personne de ton choix.

Écris au moins quatre phrases pour chacun. Si tu peux en faire plus, n'hésite pas !

3 Progresse en anglais

D. Fais ces activités en ligne pour t'entraîner et t'améliorer.

Activités de remédiation
hatier-clic.fr/21PYB86

GROUP WORK

Time to act

Design the rooms of your ideal house and present them to the class.

WB > P. 100

step 1 Imagine your house: choose the country and the place, decide the type of house or apartment, if there is a garden, a garage, etc.

step 2 Say how many rooms there are in your house. Be imaginative and creative! Every student chooses one room or two.

step 3 Say what pieces of furniture there are in your room. Cut pictures of them from a magazine or find them online. Take a shoe box and make your room. Build the house with all the boxes.

step 4 Prepare your presentation to the class. Every student talks about his or her room(s) and what he or she does there.

step 5 Present your house to the class. Be original! The houses can be presented in the school library.

Digital alternative

Record your presentation. You can use a tablet or a smartphone.

Don't forget

Grammar → p. 80
Pour indiquer la position
Pour parler de ta routine

Vocabulary → p. 82
Places in the house
Objects in the house
Daily routine
Frequency

Well done!

Now it's time to fill in your passport!

Your passport
Fiche à télécharger hatier-clic.fr/21PYB87

Trip 6 Made to play

Time to act

- Prepare a presentation to change your recess and playground habits.

Prepare your trip

Look at the photo. Say who the people are and where they are.

Watch the video and play the clapping game.
WB > P. 101 Prof 8

GROUP WORK Visit the website and say why recess is good for you. hatier-clic.fr/21PYB88

Your goals

Avec ce voyage, tu vas :

- Découvrir des cours de récréation originales, les activités que l'on peut y faire et celles qui sont interdites.
- Parler de tes activités et habitudes pendant la récréation.
- Réfléchir à comment mieux jouer ensemble dans la cour.

Students during recess in a middle school in California.

Downloads

EXTRA RESOURCES FOR TEACHERS

- → These 18 awesome school playgrounds make recess more fun than ever
- → Recycled playground ideas
- → A guide to indoor recess

ACCESS TO YOUR *digital tools*

Quest 1

School playgrounds

Quand tu regardes une vidéo, il n'est pas nécessaire de tout comprendre : concentre-toi sur l'image et les mots que tu connais déjà.

A Child's play

Parcours santé

Recess is an essential moment. It is a time to think, imagine, play and socialise. Thanks to recess, pupils are more attentive.

WB > P. 102

1. Look at the photo. Say what you see.
2. Situate all the equipment you see.

   The running track is next to the jungle gym.

3. List the activities children can do.

Grammar

- Pour parler de tes activités quotidiennes, tu utilises le présent simple :
  *At recess, I **play** soccer with my friends.*
- Pour parler d'une obligation ou d'une interdiction, utilise « *must* » ou « *must not* » / « *mustn't* ».
  *You **mustn't** run in the classroom.*

Vocabulary

talk /ɔ/
hang out with
play
stay in**side** /eɪ/ /aɪ/
have fun
sit on

school clubs
glee club /iː/
gardening club
school **ra**dio /eɪ/
recess

Prof 56 Elève 47

B Time for a break

Video

Do you play with your friends during recess?

Yes, I do!

Tips

In the US, we talk about *recess* and *soccer* but in the UK, children talk about *break time* and *football*.

1. Look at the photo. Say what you can.
2. Watch the video. Write down the recess activities. **WB > P. 102**
3. Ask your friends about their recess activities.

C Garden club rules

RULES of the GARDEN:

1 You must be responsible.

2 You must respect all plants.

3 You mustn't stand in the plant beds.

4 You mustn't play with garden tools.

1. Look at the photo. Say where the students are.
2. Read the rules of the garden and spot the students who are not respecting them.
3. Imagine four new rules for this gardening club. **WB > P. 104**

Mini challenge GROUP WORK

Present a new recess school club to the class WB > P. 105

Choose a club name and the activities you can do.
Write five rules for your club. Don't forget to use *MUST* or *MUSTN'T*.
Present your school club to the class.
Vote for the most original one!

Quest N 2

Play together

Observe les visages des personnages. Cela aide à comprendre le ton du texte.

D Play fair!

"We do not want you to play with us," said Nick.

"Why not?" asked Emma. "Because you are a girl," said Reza. "And girls do not play soccer."

✦ *Playground Problem,* by Margaret McNamara.

We don't want you to play with us, because boys don't play hopscotch.

Wrong! Boys play hopscotch too.

1. Read the texts and say what Nick and Reza think.

   Nick and Reza think girls...

2. Look at the faces and describe the kids' feelings.

3. Imagine another scene and act it out. **WB > P. 107**

Grammar

› Pour dire ce que tu veux faire, utilise *WANT TO* + base verbale.
*I **want to** play with you.*
*Emma **wants to** play football.*

› Pour dire ce que tu ne veux pas faire, utilise *DON'T WANT TO* + base verbale.
*I **don't want to** play football.*

Vocabulary

em**barr**assed /æ/ /t/
sur**prised** /aɪ/ /d/
share /eə/
play to**geth**er
in**clude** **ev**eryone /uː/
re**spect** **oth**ers /ʌð/

angry
proud
kind
friendly

Prof 57 Elève 48

E Everyone can play!

Video

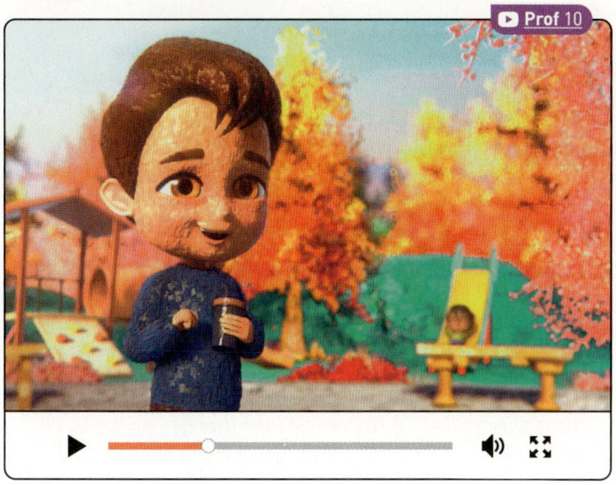

1. Watch the video and present the boy (name, place, feelings). **WB > P. 108**
2. Say what the boy wants.
3. Give three rules to include all children in the playground.

F Be a buddy, not a bully!

✦ Project created by Boys & Girls Clubs of Santa Fe del Norte.

1. Say what the object in the photo is.
2. Describe it (text, colours, symbols...).
3. Give three reasons for having a "buddy bench" in your playground. **WB > P. 110**

Tips

When you want a friend to play with or talk to, you sit on the buddy bench. A new friend will find you!

Mini challenge GROUP WORK

Write messages on your own buddy bench WB > P. 111

Choose positive messages for your buddy bench and write them down.

Decorate your bench with illustrations and colours.

Grammar break

Quiz hatier-clic.fr/21PYB94a

Pour parler de tes habitudes

WB > P. 103

Pour parler de tes habitudes, tu utilises le présent simple.

Forme affirmative	Forme négative	Forme interrogative
I / You / We / They + base verbale *He / She / It /* + base verbale-s	*I / You / We / They* + *don't* + base verbale *He / She / It /* + *doesn't* + base verbale	*Do* + *I / you / we / they* + base verbale? *Does* + *he / she / it* + base verbale?

*At recess, I **talk** with my friends.*

*Tom **plays** football.*

*My best friend **goes** to glee club.*

*They **don't go** to the school library.*

*She **doesn't go** to the gardening club.*

***Do** you **have** fun at recess?*

***Does** he **go** to the playground?*

Tuto hatier-clic.fr/21PYB94b

Exercices

WB > P. 112

1 Mets les verbes entre parenthèses au présent simple.

Ex.: At recess, I ... soccer! (play)
➡ At recess, I play soccer!

a. At recess, I ... (go) to the school library.
b. With my best friend, Zeenat, we ... on benches. (sit)
c. Zeenat is very chatty! She ... a lot. (talk)
d. On Mondays, ... you ... soccer or basketball? (play)
e. After school, Aziz ... to the gardening club but Mary and Gemma ... to glee club! (go – not go)

2 Dis si tu fais ou non ces activités à la récréation.

Ex.: sit on benches
➡ I sit / don't sit on benches.

a. play soccer
b. go to the school library
c. talk with my friends

3 Raconte le parcours d'activités de Darren à chaque récréation.

Ex.: At recess, Darren plays on the jungle gym.

a.  b.  c.  d. 

Pour parler d'obligation et d'interdiction

WB > P. 105

Pour parler d'une obligation, tu utilises *MUST* + base verbale.
Pour parler de ce qu'il est interdit de faire, tu utilises *MUST NOT* + base verbale ou, à la forme contractée, *MUSTN'T* + base verbale.

*You **must** respect your friends.*
*You **mustn't** stand in the plant beds.*

Tuto
hatier-clic.fr/21PYB95

Exercices

WB > P. 112

4 Complète les phrases avec *MUST* pour une obligation ou *MUST NOT* pour une interdiction.

*Ex.: You **mustn't** bully your school friends.*

a. You ... be a buddy.
b. We ... have fun.
c. I ... play dangerous games in the playground.
d. Children ... play with everybody at school.
e. We ... go to the garden without permission.

5 Écris les règles de la cour à Jefferson Middle School.

Ex.: have fun
➡ You must have fun!

a. stay in your running lane
b. stand in the plant beds
c. talk in the library
d. respect the playground

Pour parler de ce que tu veux faire

WB > P. 108

Pour parler de ce que tu veux, tu utilises *WANT* suivi d'un nom ou d'une base verbale précédée de *TO*.

*I **want** more benches.*
*I **want to play** with you.*

Exercices

6 Écris les équipements que tu veux ou non pour ta propre cour de récréation.

Ex.: I want a gardening club.
I don't want a shelter.

a. I ... more benches.
b. I ... a running track.
c. I ... a jungle gym.
d. I ... hopscotch.
e. I ... a soccer net.

7 Observe ce que Tom veut pour sa cour de récréation et écris-le.

Ex.: Tom wants shelters in his playground.

Vocabulary break

Pour te souvenir de tout ce vocabulaire, chante-le comme dans un *clapping game* !

WB > P. 113

Playground activities

Prof 58 Elève 49

talk /ɔ/

hang out with my friends

play **socc**er / **ba**sketball

stay in**side** /eɪ/ /aɪ/

have fun

Playground equipment

Prof 59 Elève 50

court /ɔː/

hopscotch

bench

running track

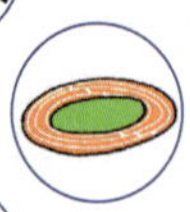

shelter /ə/

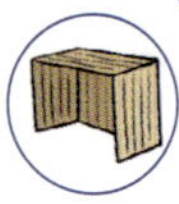

soccer net

swings

School clubs

Prof 60 Elève 51

glee club /iː/

gardening club

school **ra**dio /eɪ/

Feelings

Prof 61 Elève 52

em**barr**assed /æ/ /t/

angry

friendly

sur**prised**

Playground rules

Prof 62 Elève 53

play to**geth**er

in**clude ev**eryone /uː/

re**spect oth**ers /ʌð/

stop **bull**ying /ʊ/

Quiz
hatier-clic.fr/21PYB96

Phonology break

Pour poser des questions fermées

L'intonation d'une question fermée est toujours montante : on y répond par *YES* ou *NO*.

Do you play with your friends? ↗ *Are you in glee club?* ↗

Exercices

1 Écoute et répète les questions suivantes.
Prof 63 Elève 54
a. Do you play soccer during recess?
b. Is there a jungle gym in your playground?
c. Do you sit on benches and talk?
d. Are you a member of a school club?

2 Écoute et repère les questions fermées.
Prof 64 Elève 55
a. During recess, I play basketball.
b. Do you have fun in the playground?
c. Are there benches in your school?
d. What's the name of your school?
e. You must respect everyone.

WORD GAMES

Game 1
Time for a mime!

Say "I want to go to glee club" with one of these emotions:
embarrassed – surprised – angry – proud – friendly.

Your classmates must guess the emotion.

Game 2
Puzzling activities

Match words from each list and find the correct activity.

include	inside
have	school clubs
go to	fun
stay	with friends
hang out	others

Game 3
Word jumble

Write messages on your bench using the word bag.

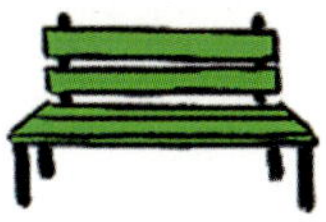

be your bully
don't respect a
fun with everybody
have
buddy friends play

Game 4
Fill in the gaps!

Find the missing letters of the following school equipment.

a. _ _ _ scotch
b. jung _ _ g _ m
c. _ _ _ cer n _ _
d. shel _ _ _
e. r _ nn _ ng tr _ c _

Time to discover

Wow! Look at these murals. They are so cool and colourful!

✦ McKinley High School Pop Art Murals, in Boston, MA
Schools often decorate their playgrounds with nice murals. Pop art is fun and accessible and the colours are bright.

✦ Thomas Buxton Primary School.

A Look at these examples of pop art murals from school playgrounds.

1. Say what these documents are and say what art style it is.
2. Think of other important words. Then practice chainspeaking with your classmates.

B Create your own pop art mural!

1. Choose an important word for your school playground.
2. Write it and illustrate it the pop art way!
3. Present your murals to the school headmaster.

Get inspired!

What is pop art?

Eleven pop art facts for kids

PAIR WORK

Time to play

IT'S TIME FOR RECESS!

Complete all eight challenges to win!

GO TO RECESS!

CHALLENGE 7
Name three things you want for your playground.

CHALLENGE 8
Give three things to write on a buddy bench.

CHALLENGE 6
Give two gardening club rules.

CHALLENGE 4
Talk about your classmate's recess habits.

CHALLENGE 5
Mime four different feelings.

CHALLENGE 3
Ask two questions about recess habits.

CHALLENGE 2
Say your favourite recess activity.

CHALLENGE 1
Name three examples of playground equipment.

- **Get into pairs. All pairs start playing at the same time.**
- **Complete all eight challenges.**
- **When you finish, say: "Stop the clock!".**
- **Recap four answers each in front of the class.**
  - If your answers are all correct, you win!
  - If one or more answers are wrong, your teacher says: "Correct challenges n°3 and 5". Start again.

Time to check

1 Vérifie tes connaissances

WB > P. 114

A. Observe et décris.

En trois minutes, écris le maximum de mots qui te viennent à l'esprit en regardant l'illustration.

2 Fais le point sur tes compétences

WB > P. 114

B. Écoute et comprends.

Audio

Prof 65 Elève 56

Écoute le discours de April, présidente du projet "*Revolutionise recess*" dans son école, et note les changements qu'elle propose avec ses camarades.

C. Parle en continu.

Parle de ton temps de récréation à l'école (présentation de la cour de récréation, règles). Dis au moins huit phrases.

3 Progresse en anglais

D. Fais ces activités en ligne pour t'entraîner et t'améliorer.

Activités de remédiation
hatier-clic.fr 21PYB100

GROUP WORK

Time to act

Change your school with the "Revolutionise recess" project. In groups, prepare a presentation to change your recess and playground habits!

WB > P. 116

step 1 Prepare your presentation and write about your school playground (equipment, recess activities and habits).

step 2 Now write about the changes you want (new equipment, activities, school clubs and rules).

Digital alternative
Make a slideshow to present your project.

step 3 Make a poster for your new project:

- Name your project.
- Draw the equipment and activities you want to add.

step 4 Write your new recess rules on the poster.

step 5 Give your presentation in front of the class.

Don't forget

Grammar → p. 94
Pour parler de tes habitudes
Pour parler d'obligation et d'interdiction
Pour parler de ce que tu veux faire

Vocabulary → p. 96
Playground activities
Playground equipment
School clubs
Feelings
Playground rules

Well done!

Now it's time to fill in your passport!

Your passport
Fiche à télécharger hatier-clic.fr 21PYB101

Trip 7 Making friends with monsters!

Time to act

- Create an exhibit for the museum of monsters and ghosts.

Prepare your trip

Look at the picture. Describe the monster and imagine what is in his mouth.

Listen to the recording and draw the monster.
WB > P. 117 Prof 66 Elève 57

Visit Tim Burton's official website. hatier-clic.fr/21PYB102

Your goals

Avec ce voyage, tu vas :

- Rencontrer de méchants et de gentils monstres et les décrire.
- Parler de ce qui est effrayant.
- Créer et exposer ton propre monstre.

Tim Burton exhibition.

Downloads

EXTRA RESOURCES FOR TEACHERS

→ How to make friends with a ghost - Read aloud

→ Tim Burton at the Museum of Modern Art (MoMa)

ACCESS TO YOUR *digital tools*

Quest 1 Meet monstrous monsters!

En regardant une vidéo, sois attentif aux bruits et aux sons.

A Monster hunting

Video

hatier-clic.fr/21PYB104

1. Watch the video and present the situation.
2. Take notes about the scary elements. **WB > P. 118**
3. Say what the girl is afraid of.

The girl is afraid of the dark.

B Dress up!

Whose red nose is it?

It is the clown's red nose!

1. Listen and point to the monsters' accessories. Prof 67 Elève 58
2. Match the accessories to the correct monster. **WB > P. 119**
3. **PAIR WORK** Ask your classmates questions about the monsters' accessories.

Grammar

- Pour demander à qui appartient un objet, utilise *WHOSE* en début de question.
  Whose hat is it?
- Pour décrire une action en cours, utilise le présent *BE* + V-*ING*.
  *The monsters **are** growling.*

Vocabulary

haunted house /ɔː/	teeth /iː/
shadows	face paint /ei/
spiders /ai/	wig
vampire /aɪə/	**broom**stick /ʊ/
werewolf /ɛə/	hat
clown /aʊ/	growl /aʊ/
witch	laugh /lɑːf/
fangs	run
cloak /əʊ/	

Prof 68 Elève 59

C There is a knock at the door!

Who's that knocking?

Who's that knocking on my door
I must admit I'm little scared,
I open it and what do I see,
A scary old witch and she's laughing at me.
Hee hee hee!

Who's that knocking at my door
I must admit I'm a little scared,
I open it and what do I see,
A green monster and he's growling at me.
GRRRR!

Now I'm walking out that door
I'm not gonna be scared no more,
I'm in my costume and I'm ready to be,
The one who's scaring you.
BOO!

1. Read the poem and pick out the monsters and their actions. **WB > P. 120**
2. Listen to the poem and read it aloud. Prof 69 Elève 60
3. Listen again to the poem and recite it.

Mini challenge GROUP WORK

Record a scary poem! **WB > P. 121**

Pick a monster or imagine a new one.

Rewrite two verses of the poem.

Put all the verses together and practice reciting your poem.

Record it.

Quest N 2

Friendly monsters

Quand tu lis un album, concentre-toi sur les images. Elles t'aideront à comprendre le texte.

D Your new best friend

✦ *How to Make Friends with a Ghost*, by Rebecca Green.

1. Look at the picture and give your first impression.
2. Use the Vocabulary box to find the missing words. **WB > P. 123**
3. Introduce your ghost to a classmate.

This is my new best friend. He has rosy cheeks.

Grammar

- Pour parler des activités qu'il est possible de faire, utilise *CAN*.
  *We **can** go for a walk today.*
- Pour parler des activités qu'il n'est pas possible de faire, utilise *CANNOT* ou *CAN'T*.
  *I **cannot (can't)** go for a walk today.*

Vocabulary

mouth /aʊ/
cheeks /tʃi:ks/
arms
fingers
body
eye /ai/
rosy /əʊ/
small
go for a walk /wɔ:k/
col**lect** leaves
go trick-or-**trea**ting /ɪ/ /i:/
read **sto**ries /i:/
eat /i:/

Prof 70 Elève 61

E Having fun with your ghost Audio

1

2

3

1. Listen to the story. Prof 71 Elève 62
2. List the activities you can do with your ghost. **WB > P. 124**
3. **PAIR WORK** Imagine three other fun activities you can do.

F You're invited! Parcours EAC

To organise a cultural event at school, create an invitation with important information, a design that your classmates will like and examples of the type of art they will see.
WB > P. 125

1. Say what this document is.
2. Read the document and pick out the information about the party (date, time, place, activities etc.). **WB > P. 125**

Mini challenge GROUP WORK

Design an invitation for a museum opening. **WB > P. 125**

Write down the important information for your event (date, time...).

Design and illustrate your invitation.

hatier-clic.fr/21PYB107

Grammar break

Quiz
hatier-clic.fr/21PYB108a

Pour parler d'une action en cours

WB > P. 121

Pour parler d'une action qui est en train de se dérouler, tu utilises le présent *BE* + V-*ING*.

The witch (Sujet) + *is* (*Be* au présent) + *laughing.* (V-*ing*)

*The monsters **are** growl**ing**.*
*The ghost **is not** fly**ing**.*

Tuto
hatier-clic.fr/21PYB108b

Exercices

WB > P. 126

1 Remets les mots dans le bon ordre.

Ex.: playing / The ghost / the piano / is / .
➡ The ghost is playing the piano.

a. I / screaming / am / at the monster / .
b. The witches / in the sky / flying / are / .
c. is / sleeping / in his coffin / not / Dracula / .
d. in the living-room / I / with / my ghost / singing / am / .
e. scary / laughing / at me / A / is / clown / .

2 Mets les verbes entre parenthèses au présent *BE* + V-*ING*.

Ex.: The witch is taking her broomstick.
She is flying now!

a. Look! The ghost ... my lunch (*eat*).
b. My friend Casper ... me with my homework (*help*).
c. My pet cat and I ... in the park with my family (*walk*).
d. Help! Seven werewolves ... outside my door (*growl*).
e. I can't believe it! I ... tennis in the living-room with my ghost (*play*).

3 Lily est très étonnée d'avoir un monstre dans sa chambre ! Utilise les mots suivants pour rédiger le SMS que Lily envoie à sa meilleure amie pour lui raconter ce qu'il est en train de faire.

video games – mango – soda
eat – drink – play

Hey Jodie! You know what, there is a monster in my room. He is …

Pour demander à qui appartient un objet

WB > P. 120

Pour demander à qui appartient quelque chose, tu utilises le mot interrogatif *WHOSE* suivi de l'objet sans article qui t'intéresse. Attention, le verbe et le pronom peuvent changer.
Whose* + nom + *is/are* + *it/they?

Si tu poses une question sur un seul objet :
Whose hat ***is it****?*

Si tu poses une question sur plusieurs objets :
Whose fangs ***are they****?*

Exercices

WB > P. 126

4 « Maman sorcière » veut que ses enfants récupèrent leurs affaires. Trouve la question qu'elle a posée à partir des réponses données.
Ex.: They are my toys.
➡ Whose toys are they?

a. It is my potion!
b. They are Tom and Tim's broomsticks.
c. It is Katie's hat.
d. They are Tom's fangs!

5 Utilise les mots suivants pour retrouver le propriétaire de chaque objet.
fangs – red nose – fur – broomstick – clown – witch – vampire – werewolf
Ex.: Whose broomstick is it? It is the witch's broomstick.

Pour parler de ce que tu peux faire

WB > P. 124

Pour parler de ce qu'il est possible de faire, utilise l'auxiliaire *CAN* suivi de la base verbale.
You ***can fly*** *with your broomstick.*

Pour parler de ce qu'il n'est pas possible de faire, utilise *CANNOT* ou *CAN'T*.
You ***can't dress up*** *as a ghost for my party.*

Exercices

6 Regarde ces images extraites de l'album sur Dawson et son ami, Ziggy the Zombie. Écris la légende sous chaque image pour expliquer ce que Dawson peut faire avec son ami.

7 Ton nouveau voisin, Igor, est un vampire. Fais la liste de toutes les activités que vous pouvez faire ensemble.
Ex.: drink red smoothies – play football at night – brush our teeth together – decorate his cloak

Igor and I can...

Vocabulary break

Pour bien mémoriser les mots, tu peux te raconter une histoire en anglais, avec les monstres et leurs accessoires.

WB > P. 127

Monsters

Prof 72 Elève 63

a witch

a **were**wolf
/ɛə/

a **vam**pire
/aɪə/

a ghost
/əʊ/

a clown
/aʊ/

Body parts

Prof 73 Elève 64

claws
/ɔː/

fur
/ɜː/

scars
/ɑː/

Feelings

Prof 74 Elève 65

scary / **spoo**ky
/ɛə/ /uː/

scared
/d/

friendly

Accessories

Prof 75 Elève 66

fangs

a cloak
/əʊ/

a hat

a wig

face paint
/eɪ/

a **broom**stick
/ʊ/

Activities

Prof 76 Elève 67

run a**way**

growl
/aʊ/

scream
/iː/

hide
/aɪ/

walk
/wɔːk/

go trick-or-**trea**ting
/ɪ/ /iː/

Quiz
hatier-clic.fr/21PYB110

Phonology break

Rhythm and rhyme

Pour réussir à lire ou à réciter un poème, il faut repérer les rimes et être attentif au rythme.

Exercices

1 Écoute le poème et repère les rimes.

Prof 77 Elève 68

My Next Door Neighbour Is A Witch

My next door neighbour is a witch,
And she lives way down in a ditch.
Her clothing is a little strange,
Because she never wants to change.

She has a black robe and a black hat,
Green skin and a smelly black cat.
A big fat wart grows on her nose,
And seventeen pimples on her toes.

2 Écoute à nouveau le poème. Récite-le en te concentrant sur le rythme de chaque vers.

WORD GAMES

Game 1

Guess who I am for Halloween

PAIR WORK Choose a costume for Halloween:

witch – werewolf – clown – vampire – green monster – ghost – zombie

Your partner must find it. Answer his / her questions.

Ex. : Have you got a red nose? – Yes, I have.
Are you green? – No I'm not.

Game 2

Monster generator

Pick a word from each category to invent a monster.

I have a spooky pink werewolf!

scary	fluffy	zombie
cute	furry	alien
spooky	pink	skeleton
friendly	slimy	werewolf

Game 3

My Halloween costume

Say what accessories you need for your costume.

Game 4

Mimes

Mime an action for your classmate to guess.

You're opening the door!

Time to discover

Monsters are not different from us after all...

✦ Australian artist Jasper St Aubyn West **transforms ordinary situations into something magical.** His monsters give more emotion to simple things with colour and a touch of humour.

A Monsters are just like us! Look at the works of art.

1. Describe the monsters (facial expressions, colours, accessories).
2. Say where they are and what they are doing.

B Now be creative! Place your monster in an everyday situation.

1. Choose a photo of an ordinary place.
2. Draw a monster and insert it into the photo.
3. Decide which work of art is very funny or very original!

Get inspired!

The Monster Project

Jasper St Aubyn West's artwork

GROUP WORK

Time to play

HAUNTED HOUSE GAME

How to play

15 min

3-4 players

The goal is to get to the attic and join your ghost!

Roll the dice and move through the house.

Count your points

Ghost room

You get an extra point!

+1 point

Monster room

To win points

Name the monster

+1 point

Name an accessory or body part

+1 point

Describe the monster's action

+1 point

Zombie room

Too bad, you lose points!

1 zombie

-1 point

2 zombies

-2 points

...

Plateau de jeu
hatier-clic.fr/21PYB113

Time to check

1 Vérifie tes connaissances

WB > P. 128

A. Observe et décris.

Regarde l'illustration ci-contre et dis tous les mots qui te viennent à l'esprit.

Joue au jeu des différences entre Ben et Bill. Il y en a cinq !

2 Fais le point sur tes compétences

WB > P. 128

B. Écoute et comprends.

Audio — Prof 78 Elève 69

Samantha se réveille et trouve un monstre dans sa chambre. Elle appelle vite son amie Gemma pour le lui dire. Écoute leur conversation, décris le monstre et tout ce qui le concerne.

C. Écris la description d'un monstre.

Fais cinq phrases pour décrire ce monstre en n'oubliant pas de dire ce qu'il est en train de faire.

3 Progresse en anglais

D. Fais ces activités en ligne pour t'entraîner et t'améliorer.

Activités de remédiation
hatier-clic.fr/21PYB114

Time to act

Create an exhibit for the museum of monsters and ghosts.

WB > P. 130

✦ Tim Burton, MoMa exhibit.

step 1 Create your monster: imagine its name, physical description, personality, accessories and actions.

step 2 Take your pens and pencils and draw your monster. Make it colourful and original.

step 3 Prepare a presentation of your monster. Take notes and ask for some help if necessary!

step 4 Practice with a classmate.

step 5 Help your teacher to prepare the exhibition.

Hang your work of art up on your classroom walls, or better yet, in the school library!

Digital alternative

When you are ready, record the presentation of your monster. Help your teacher to organise the virtual museum!

Don't forget

Grammar → p. 108

Pour parler d'une action en cours
Pour demander à qui appartient un objet
Pour parler de ce que tu peux faire

Vocabulary → p. 110

Monsters
Body parts
Feelings
Accessories
Activities

Well done!

Now it's time to fill in your passport!

Your passport
Fiche à télécharger hatier-clic.fr 21PYB115

Trip 8 Elementary London

Time to act

- Be a “London expert”: guess the names of famous monuments and places in London!

Prepare your trip

Look at the picture and name everything you recognise (places, people, means of transport...).

Listen to the recording. Prof 79 Elève 70
Say what you understand about Helena and find the monuments on the picture.

Visit the website and discover interesting facts about London. hatier-clic.fr/21PYB116

Your goals

Avec ce voyage, tu vas :

- Découvrir Londres et le Londres de Sherlock Holmes.
- Pouvoir t’orienter dans une grande ville et donner des indications.
- Poser des questions à propos de lieux.

A Different London, by Vicky Scott.

Downloads

EXTRA RESOURCES FOR TEACHERS

@ → Things to do in London
@ → Artistic London maps
@ → The Sherlock Holmes Museum
@ → Escape Game The final test

ACCESS TO YOUR *digital tools*

Quest N 1

Uncover London

N'hésite pas à demander à tes camarades de répéter ou de parler plus fort si tu ne les comprends pas !

A Fun London

Video

1. Watch the video and say what the children are talking about.
2. Pick out the activities you can do in London. **WB > P. 132**
3. Choose your favourite activity. Say why.

The London Eye looks exciting!

B Visit Bankside

1. Look at the map of Bankside and say where you can: *admire modern art / visit an old British ship / learn about Shakespeare and see one of his plays.*
2. Say what you can do at: *Borough Market / Crossbones Garden / Flat Iron Square / Bankside Pier.*
3. **GROUP WORK** Now look at the map and the other information about London. Say what fun things you can do in London. **WB > P. 133** hatier-clic.fr 21PYB118

Grammar

Pour te renseigner sur les différents monuments londoniens, tu devras poser des questions pour connaître :

- où ils se trouvent (***where...?***)
- les horaires (***what time...?***)
- les activités (***what...?***)

Vocabulary

mu**se**ums /iː/
walk
cycle /aɪ/
see
b**oa**t = ship /əʊ/
double-**deck**er bus /ʌ/
the Tube = the Under**ground** /aʊ/

m**ee**t /iː/
brilliant /ɪ/
awesome /ɔː/
im**press**ive

Prof 80 Elève 71

C Park life Parcours citoyen

Saint James's Park

Tube Stations

UNDERGROUND

Hyde Park Corner
Green Park

Park hours

Open at 5 a.m.
Closed at midnight

Attractions

Changing of the Guard
Duck Island (nature reserve)

Activities

Walk along the Mall

Meet the pelicans

1. Say all you can about St James's Park.
2. **GROUP WORK** Become an expert on London Parks: find and share information about the parks (Tube station, hours, attractions, activities). **WB > P. 135** hatier-clic.fr/21PYB119
3. Share what you know.

In July 2019, London became the first "National Park City" celebrating its biodiversity and greenness. 15,000 species live in London and there are almost as many people as there are trees.

Mini challenge

Your top three! WB > P. 135

Choose your three favourite London attractions and discuss your choices with your group. Then recap the class' three favourite attractions.

Quest N 2

In Sherlock's shoes

Sois attentif aux verbes : leur signification peut changer quand ils sont suivis d'une préposition !

D Famous Londoners

1

2

3

a

b
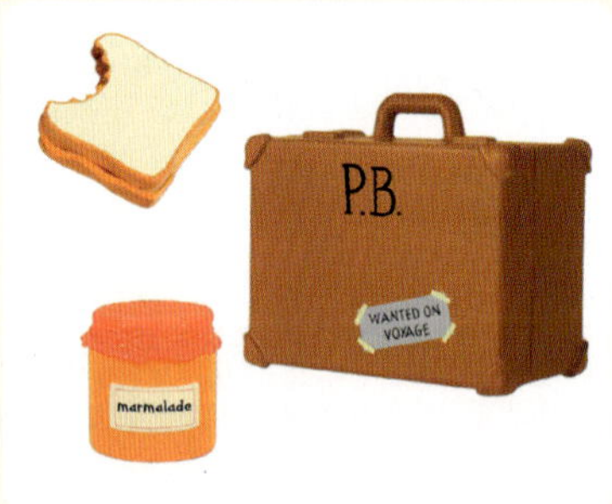

c

1. Say what you can about these famous Londoners: who are they?
2. Match the objects to the correct owner.
3. Choose the best companion for a mission in London and say why.

I think ... is the best companion because...

Grammar

Pour donner des directions, utilise l'impératif du verbe suivi d'une préposition de direction.
Turn left!
Go straight on!

Vocabulary

umbrella
suitcase /uː/
mobile /aɪ/
watch
binoculars

turn left / right /aɪ/
go straight on /eɪ/
cross
go to
wait

no entry
road closed
pedestrian zone
give way

Prof 81 Elève 72

E The game is on!

1. Read the text messages on John's phone and explain the problem.
2. Give the different steps of John's itinerary. **WB > P. 137**

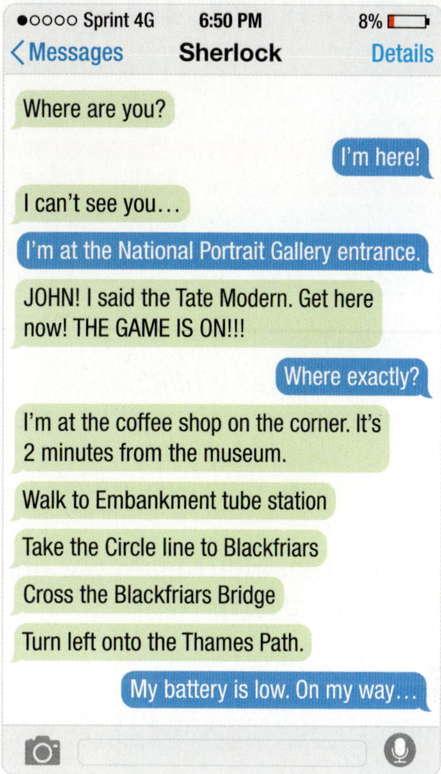

F On a mission with Sherlock! Video

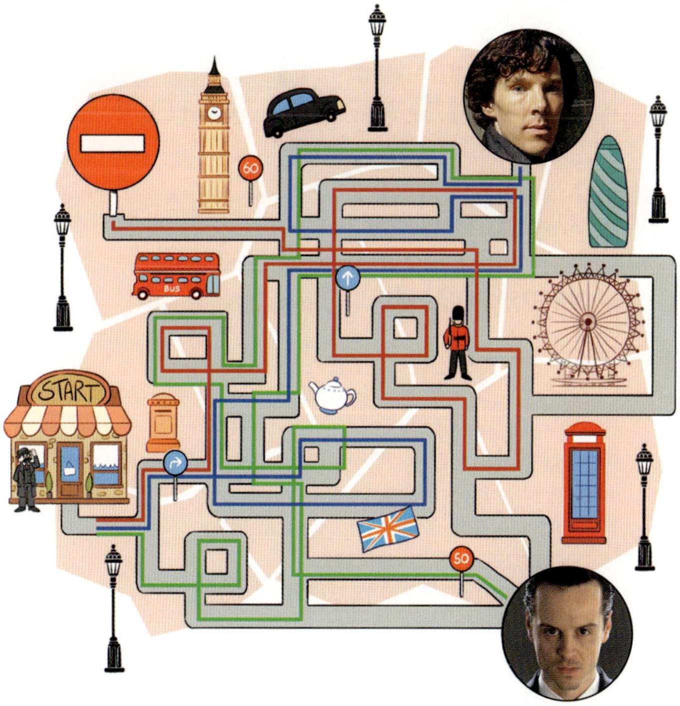

1. Watch the video and say what is special about Sherlock. Prof 12
2. Focus on all the road signs. Say what they mean. **WB > P. 138**
3. **PAIR WORK** Imagine you are Sherlock. Help John Watson find his way.

Mini challenge

Got you! WB > P. 139

You know where Moriarty is. Send John a text message. Help him find Moriarty.

Grammar break

Quiz
hatier-clic.fr/21PYB122a

Pour poser des questions

WB > P. 133

Pour poser des questions, tu peux utiliser des mots interrogatifs. Ils commencent le plus souvent par *WH-*.

Pour te renseigner sur :

- un lieu, tu utiliseras *WHERE*…
- une chose, une activité, tu utiliseras *WHAT*…
- une heure, tu utiliseras *WHAT TIME*…
- une personne, tu utiliseras *WHO*…

Tu feras suivre le mot interrogatif par un auxiliaire, un sujet et un verbe (si l'auxiliaire n'est pas *BE*).

***Where** is Regent's Park?*
***What** can you see from the London Eye?*

Tuto
hatier-clic.fr/21PYB122b

WHERE ?

WHAT ?

WHAT TIME ?

WHO ?

Exercices

WB > P. 141

1 Remets les mots de la question dans l'ordre.
Ex.: can / learn / history / Where / about / you / ?
➡ *Where can you learn about history?*

a. do / you / in / What / Regent's park / can / ?
b. Sherlock / Where / are / and Watson / ?
c. the / What / Eye / London / time / does / open / ?
d. this / Who / is / Londoner / famous / ?

2 Trouve le mot interrogatif manquant : *where, what, what time, who.*
Ex.: … is Buckingham Palace?
➡ *Where is Buckingham Palace?*

a. … does the Sherlock Holmes museum open?
b. … can you see pelicans in London?
c. … can you see at the London Dungeon?
d. … is this extraordinary woman with an umbrella?

3 Trouve la question en accord avec la réponse proposée.
Ex.: The London Dungeon opens at 10 in the morning.
➡ *What time does the London Dungeon open?*

a. St James's Park is next to Buckingham Palace.
b. It is Watson, Sherlock's companion.
c. At the Tate Modern, you can see contemporary paintings.
d. You can walk along the Mall.

Pour donner direction ou itinéraire

WB > P. 138

Pour donner des directions ou un itinéraire :

- Choisis un verbe de mouvement.
- Mets le verbe à l'impératif.
- Rajoute une préposition de direction.

***Turn** right!*

***Go** straight on.*

***Walk** to the museum.*

Exercices

WB > P. 142

4 Associe chaque illustration au bon verbe.

a.

b.

c.

d.

1. cycle 2. cross 3. walk 4. turn

5 Remets les mots de ces phrases dans l'ordre.

Ex.: to / Natural History Museum / go / the / .
➡ Go to the Natural History Museum.

a. London Eye / walk / to / the / .
b. Bridge / cross / Waterloo / .
c. turn / Oxford Street / onto / right / .
d. straight / go / on / .

6 Réécris l'itinéraire ci-dessous en remplaçant les panneaux de signalisation par des directions.

Ex : = turn left

a. To go to London Zoo from Marylebone Station, .
b. Then onto Rossmore Road.
c. onto Park Road.
d. And then into Regent's Park. The zoo is in the park!

Vocabulary break

Pour mémoriser le vocabulaire, tu peux l'organiser en carte mentale. Cela donnera une bonne vision de ce que tu as appris.

WB > P. 143

London places

Prof 82 Elève 73

mu**se**um

park

Activities and actions

Prof 83 Elève 74

see

meet

walk /ɔː/

cycle /aɪ/

cross

Transport

Prof 84 Elève 75

double-**deck**er bus /ʌ/

boat, ship /əʊ/

taxi

the Tube,
the Under**ground** /aʊ/

Directions

Prof 85 Elève 76

turn left

turn right /aɪ/

go straight (on) /eɪ/

Quiz
hatier-clic.fr/21PYB124

Phonology break

Pour poser des questions ouvertes

Lorsque tu poses une question qui commence par un mot interrogatif en *WH-*, il s'agit d'une question ouverte. L'intonation monte, puis descend.

What time does the museum open? ↗ ↘ *Where is London zoo?* ↗ ↘

Exercices

1 Écoute et répète avec la bonne intonation. Prof 86 Elève 77

a. Where are you?
b. Who is Doctor Watson?
c. What time does the London Dungeon open?
d. What can you do at Hyde Park?

2 Écoute et répète avec la bonne intonation. Dis si c'est une question ouverte ou fermée. Prof 87 Elève 78

a. Is that London zoo?
b. Where can I watch a movie?
c. Who is playing at the Royal Albert Hall?
d. Can we go to the theatre?
e. Do you like cycling in London?

WORD GAMES

Game 1
Do you know London?

Find six famous places in London.

B.P.	L.D.
N.H.M.	M.T.
L.E.	K.G.

Game 2
The odd one out

In each list, find the odd one out.

a. Sherlock Holmes – Moriarty – Paddington – Doctor Watson

b. Kensington Gardens – Trafalgar Square – St James's Park – Regent's Park

c. Tate Modern – the London Transport Museum – the National Portrait Gallery – the London Eye

Game 3
Getting around London

Read the itinerary and put the means of transport in the correct order.

a. Take a cab to Oxford Circus.

b. Take the Bakerloo line to Waterloo station.

c. Go to London Bridge by boat.

d. Take a bus to the Museum of London.

Game 4
London has no secrets for us!

Make the longest list of places to go to in London.

Pupil A: You can go to ...
Pupil B: You can go to ... and ...
Pupil C: You can go to ..., ... and ... !

Time to discover

Do you want to visit Harry Potter's London?

Of course I do!!!

a

b

c

A Look at these famous places from London and the world of Harry Potter.

1 Match each text to the right photo.
2 Say what photo does not have a description.
3 With the help of your class and your knowledge about Harry Potter, present this place.

1 ✦ A classic red phone box in London is secretly the enchanted entrance to the Ministry of Magic.

2 ✦ In *Harry Potter and the Philosopher's Stone*, Harry goes to a zoo. He sees reptiles and even speaks Parseltongue, the language of serpents!

B Now be a guide for a Harry Potter London tour.

1 Use the descriptions above to present one of the places.
2 Choose another place in London and prepare your own short presentation.

Get inspired!

The making of Harry Potter from London

GROUP WORK

Time to play

GOOSE GAME — Everything you know about London

To play, you need:

4 players

1 dice

If you land on a:

Blue square: say what can you see or do.
Orange square: say where you can see it.
Green square: say what it is.
Road sign: stop and wait your next turn.

If your answer is correct, roll again!
If it's wrong, wait your turn.

Special squares

At Buckingham Palace: the Queen invites you to dinner. Miss your turn!
At the Tower of London: you are locked in the Dungeon. Go back to square 1!
At Harrods: you do a lot of shopping. Miss 2 turns!
At Trafalgar Square: you forgot your umbrella at Madame Tussauds. Go back to circle 8!

Plateau de jeu
hatier-clic.fr/21PYB127

Time to check

1 Vérifie tes connaissances

WB > P. 144

A. Parle de monuments et lieux touristiques londoniens.

Choisis l'un des monuments ci-dessous et présente-le.

1

2

3

4

2 Fais le point sur tes compétences

WB > P. 144

B. Écoute et comprends.

Audio — Prof 88 Elève 79

Écoute cette conversation entre Jessica et Kamil. Explique la situation et leur programme d'activités.

C. Lis et comprends.

Lis l'échange de SMS suivant et repère l'itinéraire que Ramesh doit prendre : jaune, rouge, ou vert.

Hi James, I'm at the London Eye! Can I meet up with you?

Hi Ramesh, meet me at Piccadilly Circus!
Go left and cross the bridge.
Go straight on and turn right after Big Ben.
Walk straight on and turn left on Trafalgar Square.
Go straight on and it's on the left.

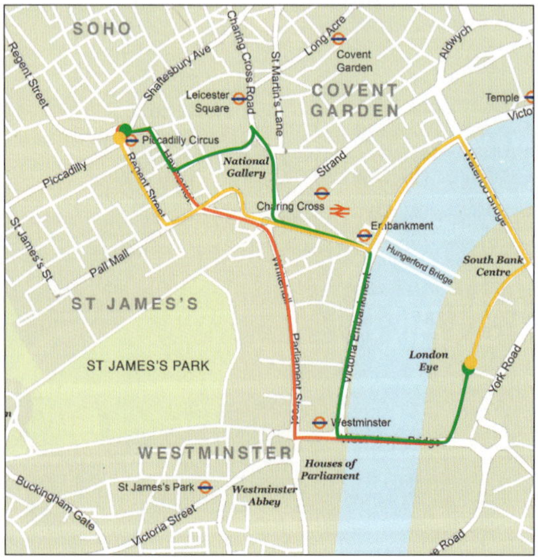

3 Progresse en anglais

D. Fais ces activités en ligne pour t'entraîner et t'améliorer.

Activités de remédiation
hatier-clic.fr 21PYB128

Time to act

Be a "London expert".

WB > P. 146

step 1 Choose a monument or a place in London.

step 2 Write down information about this monument or place:

- Tube station(s)
- Opening and closing times
- Activities

step 3 Practice your oral presentation about your monument or place.

step 4 Present your monument or place, but do not give the name.

step 5 Answer your classmates' questions about your monument or place. They must guess what it is!

Digital alternative

Record your presentation and post it on your school's digital workspace.

Your classmates comment on your post and guess the name of your monument or place.

Don't forget

Grammar → p. 122
Pour poser des questions
Pour donner direction ou itinéraire

Vocabulary → p. 124
London places
Activities and actions
Transport
Directions

Well done!

Now it's time to fill in your passport!

Your passport
Fiche à télécharger hatier-clic.fr 21PYB129

Trip 9 Be fantastic, use less plastic!

Time to act

- Make a poster to convince people to use less plastic. Present it to the class.
  WB > P. 147

Prepare your trip

Look at the photo. Describe what people are doing. Make a list of all the plastic items you can find on beaches and in the ocean.
WB > P. 147

Give a definition of plastic pollution. Say who is in danger. Prof 13

Visit the Kids Against Plastic website. Discover what happens to your plastic straws. hatier-clic.fr/21PYB130

Your goals

Avec ce voyage, tu vas :

- Dire ce que tu peux faire contre la pollution plastique.
- Parler d'une expérience qui s'est déjà déroulée.
- Agir pour la planète.

British teenagers often participate in beach cleanups.

Downloads

EXTRA RESOURCES FOR TEACHERS

- → Reduce your use of plastic
- → A speechless cartoon
- → Single-use plastic vs long-lasting solutions
- → Reducing waste

ACCESS TO YOUR *digital tools*

Quest N 1

Kids' actions

Commence par regarder le titre et la photo de l'article pour préparer ta lecture. Cela permet d'anticiper sur le contenu.

A Kids protest everywhere

Yesterday, many children and their parents were outside a Tesco supermarket in Beeston with homemade banners and bags of plastic waste. They protested for the planet, against plastic polluters, like straws and plastic cups. They explained they wanted a change because they avoided single-use plastic. Aoife Hampson, 14 was there. She explained they used tote bags instead of plastic bags. She said: "Every little thing you do can make a massive change. We want to save our future."

1. Describe the picture: say where the kids are and what they are doing. **WB > P. 148**
2. List the plastic items they refused to use.
3. Give the reasons why they protested.

Grammar

- Pour parler de quelque chose qui est passé, tu ajoutes *-ed* à la fin du verbe ou *-d* si la base verbale se termine par un E.
- Pour faire le lien entre ses idées, tu utilises de petits mots qui relient les phrases entre elles, comme *AND*, *BUT* ou *BECAUSE*.

Vocabulary

po**llu**ter /uː/
single-**use** /juː/
str**aw** /ɔː/
c**u**p /ʌ/
bottle cap
w**a**ter **bott**le /ɔː/
banner /æ/
pick up
take **ac**tion
re**cy**cle /aɪ/
co**llect**
do**nate**
a**void**
re**duce** /i/ /juː/
in**stead** of /e/

Prof 89 Elève 80

B Amy and Ella, founders of Kids Against Plastic

Video

hatier-clic.fr/21PYB133

1. Look at the title and at the photo. Guess who the two girls are.
2. Look at their clothes. Imagine what they are talking about.
3. Watch the video.
   - List the big four plastic polluters. **WB > P. 149**
   - Say what single-use plastic is.
   - Recap what Ella and Amy decided.

C You can reduce plastic!

1. Read the text in the poster.
2. Make five sentences to say what YOU did last week to reduce plastic waste. **WB > P. 149**

Ex.: Last week, I used reusable water bottles.
Last week, I avoided plastic containers.

Mini challenge GROUP WORK

Apply for 'Kids Against Plastic' WB > P. 150

Like Amy and Ella, you want to take part in 'Kids against plastic' organisation. Draw a T-shirt and imagine a slogan against plastic pollution for the conference. Then write a short email to explain your last week actions against plastic pollution.

We must protect turtles from plastic pollution.

Last week, I cleaned beaches with my friends.

Quest 2 A plastic-free party

Pour décrire une image, commence par décrire l'ensemble en t'aidant du titre avant de rentrer dans les détails.

D Let's organise a party! Parcours culturel

1. Describe this poster and say what you understand from the slogan. WB > P. 152
2. Say what is necessary for a plastic-free party.

Many teenagers take a packed lunch to eat at school. It typically consists of a sandwich, a packet of crisps, some fruit and a drink - often fizzy and in a plastic bottle.

Yes! And the packed lunch is usually plastic-wrapped.

WB > P. 153

What can I do to organise a plastic-free party?

Well... Let's make homemade chocolate cakes instead of plastic-wrapped cookies!

Grammar

- Pour faire une suggestion, tu peux utiliser ***LET'S*** devant la base verbale et avoir une intonation enthousiaste.
  Let's decorate!
- Pour inciter quelqu'un à ne pas faire quelque chose, tu places ***DON'T*** avant la base verbale.
  Don't use plastic!

Vocabulary

- scrap-**pa**per chain /eɪ/
- pompom puff /ʌ/
- **sal**ad bowls /əʊ/
- ce**ram**ic plates /eɪ/
- glass **bott**les
- **ta**blecloth
- bal**loon** /bəˈluːn/
- home**made** /eɪ/
- **plas**tic-free /iː/

Prof 90 Elève 81

E How to organise a plastic-free birthday party

Audio

Let's organise a plastic-free party!

Great idea! But what can we do?

1. Listen to the audio. Say why it is important to avoid plastic. Prof 91
2. List the different tips to organise a plastic-free party. **WB > P. 153**
3. Say what else you can do.

F Don't use plastic!

1. Describe the picture. Say why Amy looks so surprised.
2. Make six sentences to suggest what is eco-friendly and what is not in this birthday party. **WB > P. 154**

Mini challenge GROUP WORK

Are you plastic clever? WB > P. 155

Draw an object.

Your team must guess the word and make a sentence with ***LET'S*** or ***DON'T*** as quickly as possible.

Be quick to score the maximum points!

It's a tote bag! Let's use a tote bag instead of a plastic bag!

Grammar break

Quiz
hatier-clic.fr/21PYB136a

Pour parler d'une expérience passée

WB > P. 149

Pour parler de quelque chose qui est passé et terminé, tu utilises le prétérit. Avec les verbes réguliers, c'est assez facile ! À la forme affirmative, tu ajoutes *-ED* ou *-D* s'il y a déjà un *E* à la base verbale.

*The kids protest**ed** against plastic bags.*
*They encourage**d** the public to refuse food packages.*

Tuto
hatier-clic.fr/21PYB136b

Pour préciser quand cette action s'est passée, tu ajoutes des marqueurs de temps.

- Lorsque cela s'est déroulé le jour précédent, tu emploies *YESTERDAY*.

  ***Yesterday**, I prepar**ed** a plastic-free lunch.*

- Lorsque c'était la semaine dernière, le mois dernier, l'année dernière, tu mets *LAST* devant le nom.

  ***Last** month, I collect**ed** ten plastic cups.*

- Enfin, pour indiquer depuis combien de temps l'action s'est passée, tu utilises *AGO*. Attention ! Il se place après la durée (days, months, years…).

PAST ☑  PRESENT

*Ten days **ago**, I clean**ed** the beach.*
*One month **ago**, I refus**ed** plastic straws at a party.*
*Last week, I pick**ed** up plastic bottles on the beach.*
*Seven days ago, I pick**ed** up plastic bottles.*

⚠ Avec le verbe *BE*, c'est différent. Tu utilises *WAS* au singulier (*I, He-She-It*) et *WERE* au pluriel (*We, You, They*).

*Yesterday my best friend **was** at a plastic-free birthday party.*
*Two months ago, my parents **were** at the supermarket and refused plastic bags.*

Exercices

WB > P. 157

1 Complète les phrases avec *BE* au prétérit (forme affirmative).

Ex.: Ella / with the supermarket manager.
*➡ Ella **was** with the supermarket manager.*

a. Keanu and Amy / on the beach.
b. You / at Tesco.
c. We / in the park.
d. Amy / in the living-room.

2 Commence les phrases par *Yesterday*.

Ex.: I collect bottle caps.
*➡ **Yesterday** I collect**ed** bottle caps.*

a. Amy and Ella refuse to use plastic.
b. The kids return plastic packaging.
c. You organise a plastic-free party.
d. We clean the park.
e. I collect bottle caps.

3 Raconte ce qu'Amy et Ella ont fait.

Ex.:  ***Last** week, Amy reus**ed** her plastic bottle.*

a. 

b. 

c. 

d. 

e. 

Pour associer les idées entre elles

Lorsque tu racontes quelque chose, tu as parfois besoin d'associer des idées entre elles. Utilise alors ces petits mots que sont les conjonctions de coordination.

- ***AND*** relie deux idées ou deux éléments.

*We make paper chains **and** homemade banners.*

- ***BUT*** oppose deux idées.

*You can't recycle a plastic bag **but** you can reuse a tote bag.*

- ***BECAUSE*** explique une idée.

*There is plastic pollution **because** people use too many single-use plastic bottles.*

Exercices

4 Choisis la conjonction qui convient le mieux pour associer les idées entre elles.
Ex.: Sea turtles are in danger. Sea turtles eat plastic bags.
➡ Sea turtles are in danger because they eat plastic bags.

a. There is plastic pollution. We can clean.
b. I've got plastic cups. I've got plastic straws.
c. Amy and Ella take action. The planet is in danger.
d. They protested against the big polluters. They protested against single-use plastic.

5 Imagine ce que Keanu a fait pour la planète. Utilise les verbes ci-dessous et des conjonctions pour associer tes idées. Fais au moins trois phrases, chacune avec une conjonction différente.
Ex.: Keanu protected the turtles and the whales.

protect recycle use pick up pollute

Pour suggérer de faire quelque chose

WB > P. 154

Lorsque tu veux inviter quelqu'un à faire quelque chose avec toi, tu dis *LET'S*, puis tu utilises la base verbale de ton choix. *LET'S* est la contraction de *LET US*.

Si tu veux l'inciter à ne pas faire quelque chose, tu emploies *DON'T* devant la base verbale.

Let's protect turtles! Don't pollute the ocean!!

Exercices

WB > P. 158

6 À partir des dessins, suggère les activités suivantes à tes amis.

Ex.:  ***Let's** make pompom puffs!*

a. 

b. 

c. 

7 Aide Keanu à organiser son anniversaire. Réponds à ses questions en l'invitant à faire autre chose.

 I've got plastic balloons.

Don't use plastic balloons! Let's make banners to decorate the room! 

a. 

b. 

c. 

d. 

e. 

Vocabulary break

Les noms composés associent deux mots qui permettent d'en faire un nouveau. Repère-les dans cette page et trouves-en de nouveaux.

WB > P. 159

Everyday objects

Prof 92 Elève 82

bottle 

fork 

plate /eɪ/ 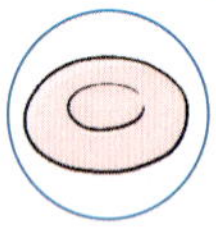

bowl /əʊ/ 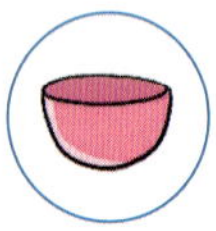

cup 

straw /ɔː/ 

tablecloth 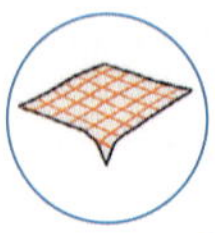

tote bag 

gift 

banner 

Adjectives

Prof 93 Elève 83

plastic-free /iː/ 

plastic-wrapped 

single-use 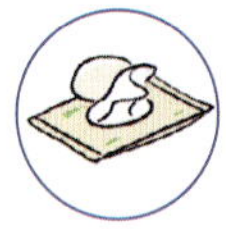

home**made** /eɪ/ 

Actions

Prof 94 Elève 84

re**duce** /juː/ 

re**cycle** /aɪ/ 

co**llect** 

throw a**way** 

do**nate** /eɪ/ 

a**void** /ɔɪ/ 

Quiz
hatier-clic.fr/21PYB138

Phonology break

Prononcer le *-ed* du prétérit

La terminaison *-ed* a trois prononciations différentes.

- Le plus souvent, tu la prononces /d/.
  *Many teenagers **refused** to use plastic bags. They **explained** they were concerned for the planet.*
- Tu prononces /t/ lorsque le verbe se termine par les sons /p/, /k/, /f/, /s/, /t/, /ʃ/ ou /tʃ/.
  *Keanu **watched** (/t/) documentaries about the big polluters. Then he **stopped** (/t/) using plastic.*
  *He **washed** (/t/) his reusable bottle and it **worked** (/t/).*
- Enfin, tu la prononces /id/ après les sons /d/ et /t/.
  *Emmy and Ella **decided** (/id/) to take action.*
  *They **started** (/id/) their project because they **wanted** (/id/) to protect the planet.*

Exercices

1 Écoute, répète et entraîne-toi. Prof 95 Elève 85

a. We reused plastic bottles.
b. I protested against the use of plastic bags.
c. They surfed among plastic bottles.
d. Then they relaxed on the beach.

2 Trouve la base verbale de ces verbes au prétérit. Puis écoute pour vérifier tes réponses. Prof 96 Elève 86

Ex. : protested ➡ protest

a. collected b. reduced c. donated d. reused
e. watched f. cleaned g. refused h. avoided
i. decided j. stopped

WORD GAMES

Game 1
The plastic chain

Look at the picture.

Name an element in the picture. The next person repeats the word and adds a new one. If it's not a new word, you lose.

Ex. : In the belly of the whale there is a spoon, a lunchbox...

Game 2
I spy with my little eye...

Look at the picture activity F on p. 135.

Ask questions to your classmate.
He / She must answer very quickly.
You win when you've got eight objects.

Pupil A: I spy with my little eye something yellow.

Pupil B: It's a plastic balloon.

Pupil A: I spy with my little eye something beginning with the letter... C.

Pupil B: It's a chocolate cake.

Time to discover

Plastic can become art!

✦ Sue Lipscombe sculpted this whale from wood and 70,000 old plastic bottles. She displayed it in Bristol.

✦ *Priscilla the Parrot Fish*. The artists of the Washed Ashore Project picked up waste, washed it and created colourful sculptures.

A Describe and comment on the two pictures.

1 Describe the sculptures (colours, items).

2 Say what the artists wanted to express.

B Now you're the artist! GROUP WORK

1 Pick up plastic waste. Wash it and bring it to school.

2 Use it with your classmates' items to make a piece of art.

3 Write a short presentation of the work: the name, the material you used...

4 Create a public art display. Place the display somewhere prominent in the school to incite discussion and spread awareness.

Get inspired! All sorts of plastic can be recycled!

Hokusai's "The Great Wave" made of plastic caps

"Gumdrop" turns recycled gum into shoes

GROUP WORK

Time to play

I put the cereal box in the paper bin.

Are you recycling right?

Put the items below in the right bin.

Plateau de jeu
hatier-clic.fr/21PYB141

Time to check

1 Vérifie tes connaissances

WB > P. 160

A. Observe et décris.

Keanu veut organiser son anniversaire sans plastique. Regarde l'image et donne-lui des conseils.

Let's use metal forks!
Don't use plastic forks!

2 Fais le point sur tes compétences

WB > P. 160

B. Lis et comprends.

Consulte le blog d'Amy. Relève les six actions qu'elle a menées en précisant bien quand elle les a réalisées.

C. Écris pour expliquer.

Envoie maintenant un message à ton ou ta camarade pour lui dire ce que tu as fait le mois dernier pour réduire ta consommation de plastique. En t'aidant de l'image, fais cinq phrases pour dire ce que tu as fait.

Amy's blog — My actions last week against plastic pollution

After watching a documentary on TV last month, I realised that I used too much plastic in my everyday life. I decided to take actions to reduce my plastic consumption.
For example, last week, I reused my old teeshirts to make a tote bag. I decided to go shopping with this new tote bag instead of using plastic bags. For my best friend's birthday last weekend, I cooked a homemade chocolate cake instead of buying packaged sweets. I also created homemade banners for the party. Two days ago, at home, I replaced plastic straws by metal straws to drink my Coke. Finally, yesterday, I convinced my parents to switch from plastic bottles to glass bottles.

3 Progresse en anglais

D. Fais ces activités en ligne pour t'entraîner et t'améliorer.

Activités de remédiation
hatier-clic.fr 21PYB142

Time to act

Make a poster to convince your classmates to use less plastic.

WB > P. 162

step 1 Find an attractive title.
Here is an example:
Let's be fantastic, use less plastic!

step 2 Write a sentence to explain why we must reduce our plastic waste.

step 3 Find three facts about the UK and plastic waste last year.
Help: https://www.recyclingbins.co.uk/recycling-facts/

step 4 Give eight pieces of advice to reduce plastic waste (let's… / don't…).
Make your poster attractive with illustrations (drawings, photos, infographics).

Digital alternative

Use CANVA (www.canva.com) to make infographics or Genially (www.genial.ly) to make an interactive poster.

step 5 Present your poster to the class. Be persuasive!
The most convincing poster will be displayed in the classroom.

Don't forget

Grammar → p. 136
Pour parler d'une expérience passée
Pour associer les idées entre elles
Pour suggérer de faire quelque chose

Vocabulary → p. 138
Everyday objects
Adjectives
Actions

Well done!

Now it's time to fill in your passport!

Your passport
Fiche à télécharger hatier-clic.fr 21PYB143

Trip 10 Little Inventors

Time to act

- Present a project for the 'Power of Children' awards.

Prepare your trip

Look at the photo.
Say what the characters are doing.
WB > P. 163

Watch the video. hatier-clic.fr/21PYB144a
Say what Hero's invention is and what it does.

Visit the website. hatier-clic.fr/21PYB144b
Say what your favourite invention is and why.

Your goals

Avec ce voyage, tu vas :

- Découvrir comment toi ou tes camarades pouvez aider à changer le monde.
- Parler de ce que tu feras dans le futur.
- Comprendre les besoins des autres et proposer une aide.

Wallace and Gromit and their brand new invention.

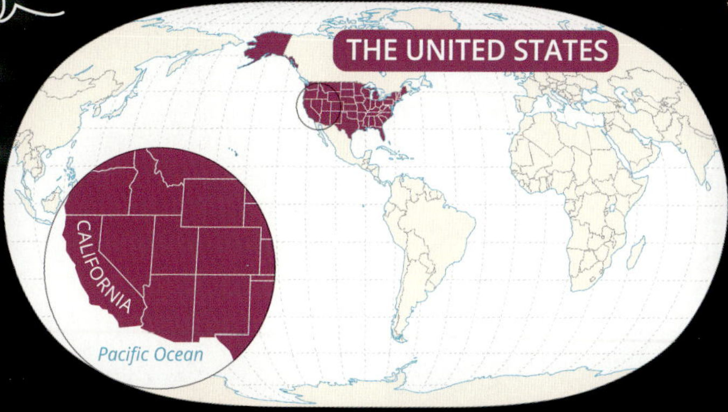

Downloads

EXTRA RESOURCES FOR TEACHERS

- → Tadashi invents Bay Max
- → Escape Game The Crab machine
- → Silicon Valley companies map

ACCESS TO YOUR *digital tools*

Quest 1

Be inventive!

A A helpful invention

Video

hatier-clic.fr/21PYB146

1. Watch the video. Say what you can see in Tadashi's workshop. **WB > P. 164**
2. **GROUP WORK** Imagine what his invention will be.
3. Now discover Tadashi's fantastic invention. **WB > P. 165**
4. Explain how Baymax will help other people.

Grammar

- Pour parler du futur, tu emploies ***WILL*** (ou ***'LL***, forme contractée) + la base verbale.
  *He **will** / He**'ll** save people.*
- À la forme négative, tu utilises ***WILL NOT*** (ou ***WON'T***, forme contractée) + la base verbale.
  *We **will not** / We **won't** need a spaceship.*

Vocabulary

in**vent** = cre**ate** /eɪ/
build /ɪ/
re**pair** = fix
heal = cure /iː/ /jʊə/
take care of
need /iː/

change
generate **en**ergy
elec**tric**ity = power
battery
turn
wheel

Prof 97 Elève 87

B My crazy invention!

I will use the wind to recharge it.

I'll create an app to recharge it.

✦ *My Crazy Inventions Sketchbook*, by Lisa Reagan. Illustrations by Andrew Rae.

1. Explain how this invention recharges the mobile phone. **WB > P. 165**
2. **PAIR WORK** Imagine your own invention to recharge the mobile. Present it to the class.

C Will we? Or won't we?

Video

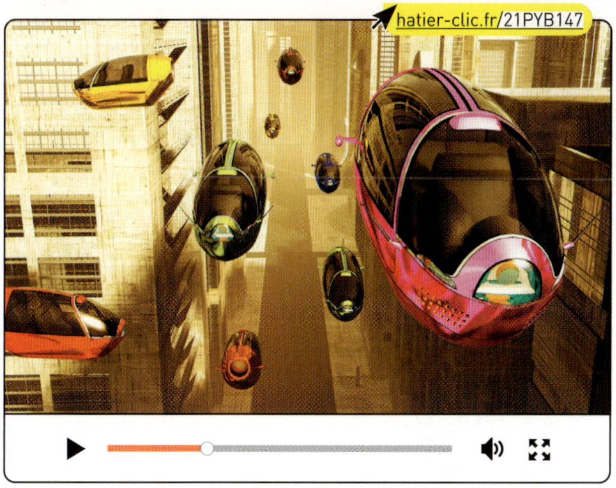

1. List the inventions in the video and say what they have in common. **WB > P. 165**
2. Say where you will go in your flying car.
3. Say what we will need to live on the moon.

Mini challenge

Imagine an invention that will help you in your everyday life **WB > P. 167**

Describe how the machine will work
and how it will help people.
Say what it won't change.

My machine will change colours.

But it won't repair a broken skateboard!

Quest 2 There's no "I" in team

N'hésite jamais à demander de l'aide à quelqu'un d'autre. Propose aussi ton aide, si quelqu'un en a besoin.

D Kid of the Year

"Observe, brainstorm, research, build and communicate." That is what Gitanjali Rao says about the process of invention. She's a young scientist, born in 2005. She won the award for TIME's Kid of the Year. Gitanjali was selected among 5000 other candidates. She uses technology to combat problems including dirty drinking water and bullying on social networks. She wants to create a group of little inventors who will solve problems everywhere on the planet. She has a motivating message: you won't fix every problem, just concentrate on one that will generate passion in you. "If I can do it," she said, "anybody can do it."

Gitanjali is very inspiring.

She's going to help many people.

1. Describe the different steps in Gitanjali's process of invention. **WB > P. 168**
2. List the problems she helped with and find their common solution.
3. Explain what Gitanjali means when she says "If I can do it, anybody can do it."
4. Imagine the job she would like to do when she is an adult.

Grammar

Pour parler de tes projets dans l'avenir, tu peux utiliser les structures suivantes : *WANT TO* + base verbale / *WOULD LIKE TO* + base verbale / *PLAN TO* + base verbale.

*I **want to** be an engineer.*
*I **would like to** be a nurse.*
*I **plan to** go to university.*

Vocabulary

a **fire**man/men /aɪə/
a n**ur**se /ɜː/
a me**chan**ic
a **sci**entist /aɪ/
a volun**teer** /ɪə/
homeless people
organi**sa**tion = **char**ity
toiletries

im**prove** life /uː/ /aɪ/
helpful /ʊ/
generous
study
in**spi**ring /aɪ/
am**bi**tious
get in**volved** in **some**thing /vd/

Prof 98 Elève 88

E A heart of gold

Video

Prof 14

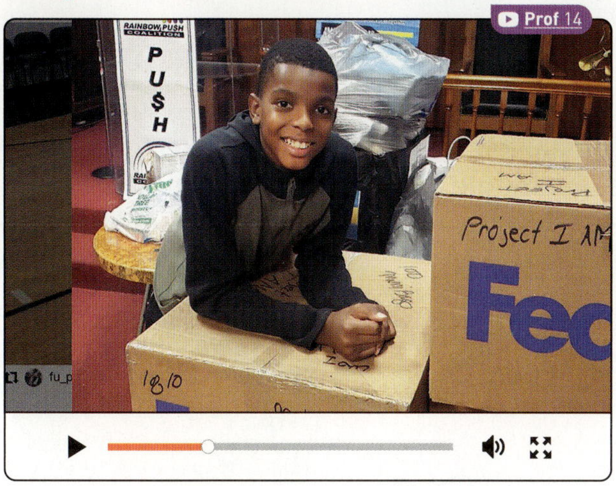

1. Watch the video. Say who Jahkil Jackson's organisation wants to help. WB > P. 168
2. Describe what a "Blessing Bag" is.
3. List the adjectives Jahkil uses to describe what emotions his project inspires.
4. Identify Jahkil's projects for the future, for himself and for his organisation.

F A helping hand

Parcours avenir

1

2

3

4

a

b

c

d

1. Look at the pictures. Explain who is going to help. Match the problem with the solution. WB > P. 170
2. Find other jobs to help people.

We won't all be rockstars or sporting heroes, but we can all help other people. Start thinking about the work experience you would like to do in year 9.
WB > P. 170

Mini challenge

Dear Future, ... WB > P. 171

Write a letter to yourself and say what you would like to be when you grow up.
Explain what you want to do or don't want to do.
Illustrate your letter.

Grammar break

Quiz
hatier-clic.fr/21PYB150a

Pour parler du futur

WB > P. 166

Pour parler de l'avenir, tu peux utiliser le modal ***WILL***. Comme ***CAN*** ou ***MUST***, ***WILL*** est toujours suivi d'une base verbale. Il est invariable à toutes les personnes.

*I **will** go.* *She **will** go.*
*You **will** go.* *They **will** go.*

- À l'oral, ***WILL*** peut se contracter sous la forme ***'LL*** : *I **will** play.* = *I**'ll** play.*
- À la forme négative, ***WILL*** devient ***WON'T*** : *I **will not** play.* = *I **won't** play.*

Tuto
hatier-clic.fr/21PYB150b

Exercices

WB > P. 173

1 Imagine trois choses que la machine de la mascotte va faire et ne va pas faire. Formule trois phrases à l'aide des mots suivants.
fly to the moon – give me good grades – change the world – swim like a fish – take care of people – fix objects – do the housework – tidy my bedroom – wash my clothes – heal terrible wounds

Ex.: Her machine will tidy my bedroom but it won't prepare coffee.

2 Observe bien les propositions suivantes et remets les mots de la phrase dans l'ordre.
Ex.: will / new / machine / create / a / Tadashi / .
➡ Tadashi will create a new machine.

a. in / bikes / flying / will / ride / future / people / the / .
b. objects / fix / ? / will / robots
c. a / won't / machine / create / I / dangerous / .
d. won't / have / a / nice / but it / will / I / pollute / car / .

3 Écris cinq phrases pour expliquer comment les gens se déplaceront en 2050.
Ex.: In 2050, people will fly to the moon.

Pour exprimer tes souhaits et tes projets

WB > P. 169

Pour dire ce que tu souhaiterais faire, tu utilises *WOULD LIKE TO* + base verbale.
Cette structure est invariable à toutes les personnes.

*He **would like to** become a mechanic.*
*They **would like to** fly.*

Pour dire ce que tu veux faire, tu utilises : *WANT TO* + base verbale.
Pour dire ce que tu prévois de faire, tu utilises : *PLAN TO* + base verbale.
Ces deux formes verbales se conjuguent au présent simple.

*In the future, I **plan to** make a difference.*
*Jahkil **wants to** stop homelessness thanks to his project.*

	Forme affirmative	*Forme négative*	*Forme interrogative*	*Réponse brève*
I You We They	*want to + BV*	*don't want to + BV*	*Do you want to + BV?*	*Yes, we do.* *No, we don't.*
She He It	*wants to + BV*	*doesn't want to + BV*	*Does she want to + BV?*	*Yes, she does.* *No, she doesn't.*

Exercices

WB > P. 173

4 Utilise un élément de chaque colonne pour écrire des phrases correctes.
Ex : I + would like to + play golf in Scotland.

I Jahkil Baymax Keanu and Amy	wants to would like to don't plan to	stop helping people. play golf in Scotland. help sick people. fly to the moon.

5 À partir des images ci-dessous, écris ce que les personnages voudraient faire dans le futur. Utilise la forme verbale qui convient le mieux.
Ex.:  *2035 ➡ He wants to / would like to / plans to buy a house in 2035.*

a.  / New York /  2030
b.  2032
c. 

Pour exprimer tes intentions

WB > P. 171

Pour exprimer ce que tu as l'intention de faire dans un futur proche ou plus lointain, tu utilises ***BE GOING TO*** + base verbale. ***BE*** se conjugue au présent.

Exercices

WB > P. 174

6 Dis ce que ces personnes ont l'intention de faire. Attention aux sujets !
Ex.: We / not / create a new machine
➡ We are not going to create a new machine.

a. Jahkil / help homeless people.
b. I / not / live in a big city.
c. What sport / you / play this weekend?
d. They / help their neighbours.

7 Compare les agendas de Keanu et d'Amy. Dis ce qu'ils vont faire cette semaine.
Ex.: Keanu is going to cook pasta on Wednesday. Amy isn't going to cook pasta on Wednesday.

Vocabulary break

Aide-toi de ce vocabulaire pour réaliser les activités du workbook.

WB > P. 175

Inventing

Prof 99 Elève 89

in**vent** 

cre**ate** /ieɪ/ 

use 

change 

build /ɪ/ 

re**pair** 

robot 

Jobs

Prof 100 Elève 90

fireman /aɪə/ 

nurse /ɜː/ 

plumber /ˈplʌm/ 

me**chan**ic /kæ/ 

guide dog 

scientist /aɪ/ 

Personality

Prof 101 Elève 91

helpful 

kind /aɪ/ 

com**pass**ionate 

in**spi**ring /aɪ/ 

am**bi**tious 

Assistance

Prof 102 Elève 92

im**prove** life /uː/ /aɪ/ 

fix objects 

heal /iː/ 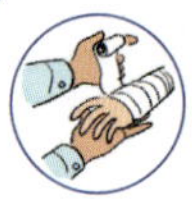

cure /jʊ/ 

help 

take care of /eɪ/ 

get in**volved** in something 

Quiz
hatier-clic.fr/21PYB152

Phonology break

Parler anglais, c'est accentuer !

L'anglais est une langue très rythmée. Certaines syllabes sont accentuées alors que d'autres ne le sont pas. Les syllabes non accentuées sont moins appuyées.

Prof 103 Elève 93

All I **want** is a **pro**per **cup** of **cof**fee,
Made in a **pro**per **cop**per **cof**fee **pot**
I **may** be **off** my **dot**
But I **want** a **cup** of **cof**fee
From a **pro**per **cof**fee **pot**.

Exercices

1 Écoute ce poème et entraîne-toi à accentuer les bonnes syllabes pour créer un rythme. Prof 104 Elève 94

Watch it. See it.
Think it. Make it.
I imagine it will be.
Design it. Build it
Glue it. Use it.
I improve things I see.

Start it. Stop it.
Try it. Fix it.
This is my new creation.
Sell it. Work it.
Heal it. Cure it.
I am an inspiration.

2 À ton tour, écris deux autres vers de ce poème en utilisant le vocabulaire de la leçon. Lis tes vers à haute voix en respectant le rythme initial.

WORD GAMES

Game 1

Ready, steady, draw!

Draw a job for your classmate.
He / She will guess what job it is.

Pupil A: Is it a nurse?

Pupil B: Yes, it is !

Game 2

Guess what my job will be!

Describe the job you would like to do in the future, your classmates must find it.

Pupil A: I would like to fix broken cars.

Pupil B: Do you want to be a mechanic?

Game 3

Black or White!

Find a synonym or an antonym

Ex. : kind = compassionate
useless ≠ helpful

a. selfish ≠ ...

b. invent = ...

c. cure = ...

d. break ≠ ...

e. nice = ...

Game 4

Add one more!

Repeat what your classmates say, and finish the sentence: "In 2030 I am going to..."

Pupil A: In 2030 I'm going to live in Wales,

Pupil B: In 2030, I'm going to live in Wales, be a teacher

Pupil C: In 2030, I'm going to live in Wales, be a teacher, have a dog, etc...

Time to discover

Art can help change the world.

✦ *Education is not a crime*. Dave the Chimp is a street artist. He represents orange "Human-beans". There is a great solidarity between these funny characters. Dave the Chimp likes to insert inspiring messages. His art can help people remember that they have the power to act and change the world.

A Look at the pictures.

1. Describe what the characters are doing.
2. Find the common themes in the messages.
3. Choose your favourite message.

B Choose an inspiring message and create your work of art.

1. Decide what message you want to share with your class.
2. Imagine some funny and simple characters that help each other.
3. Create the drawing alone or with a friend of yours.
4. Present your artwork to your classmates.

Get inspired!

Inspiring quotes

Learn more about Dave the Chimp

GROUP WORK

Time to play

Build a Fortune Telling Machine

1. Write down eight different possible "futures" for your friends.
2. Use "will", "won't", "are going to...", "aren't going to"
3. Add the colours and numbers.
4. Play and tell the future.

You are going to be rich.

You won't go to Australia.

You will win the world cup.

You aren't going to fly to Mars.

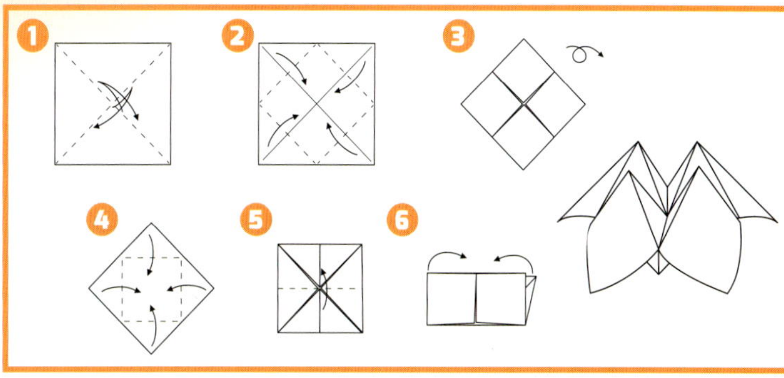

Time to check

1 Vérifie tes connaissances

WB > P. 176

A. Observe l'image et dis quelles seront les fonctionnalités de ce robot.

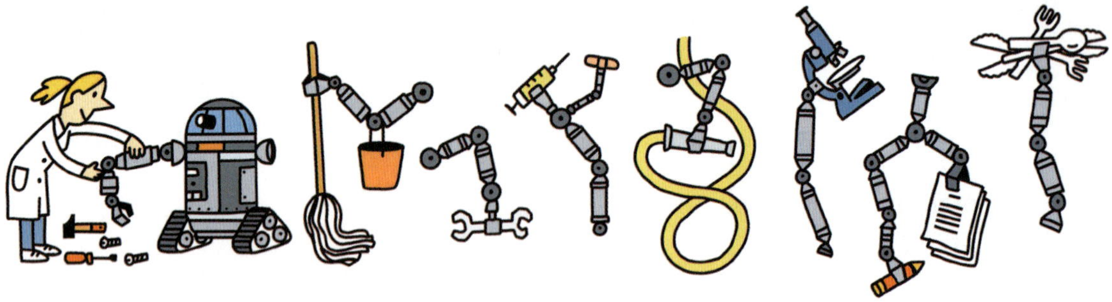

2 Fais le point sur tes compétences

WB > P. 176

B. Écoute et comprends.

Audio — Prof 105 Elève 95

Écoute ces deux élèves de 3e discuter avec leur professeur de leur futur stage en entreprise. Dis quels métiers les intéressent et pourquoi.

C. Lis et comprends.

Lis ce texte et :

- Décris le problème constaté par le jeune inventeur.
- Explique l'invention.
- Dis ce que l'invention a changé.

I'm very happy to accept my young inventor's award today. My parents often buy plants for the house but the plants often die very quickly. We all know that plants need water, not everyday, but regularly. In my family, everybody, didn't remember to water them. My application will now send a message to everyone in the family. It will tell them to water the plants. Thanks to the app, the plants will live longer. There will be more oxygen in the atmosphere and our house will be more beautiful.

3 Progresse en anglais

D. Fais ces activités en ligne pour t'entraîner et t'améliorer.

Activités de remédiation
hatier-clic.fr/21PYB156

Time to act

You're the candidate for this year's 'Power of Children' awards. Present your project.

WB > P. 178

step 1 Explain the situation you would like to change.

step 2 Describe the actions you will take to make a change.

step 3 Expose the changes you would like to see thanks to your project.

step 4 Create a poster to promote and illustrate your action.

> **Digital alternative**
> Create a video to present your project to the jury.

step 5 Present your project to the class.

Don't forget

Grammar → p. 150
Pour parler du futur
Pour exprimer tes souhaits et tes projets
Pour exprimer tes intentions

Vocabulary → p. 152
Inventing
Jobs
Personality
Assistance

Well done!

Now it's time to fill in your passport!

Your passport
Fiche à télécharger hatier-clic.fr 21PYB157

Time to celebrate HALLOWEEN

A Put on your scary costume!

1. Say everything you know about Halloween.
2. Say what the Louds are wearing.
3. Say what your favourite costume is.

Prof 106

Halloween is on October 31st and everyone gets dressed as a ghost, a witch or something scary. It originally comes from Ireland. Irish immigrants took their traditions with them when they moved to the United States. Today it is one of the most popular celebrations of the year... and not just in the USA. Adults and children all have fun on this ~~day~~.... night!

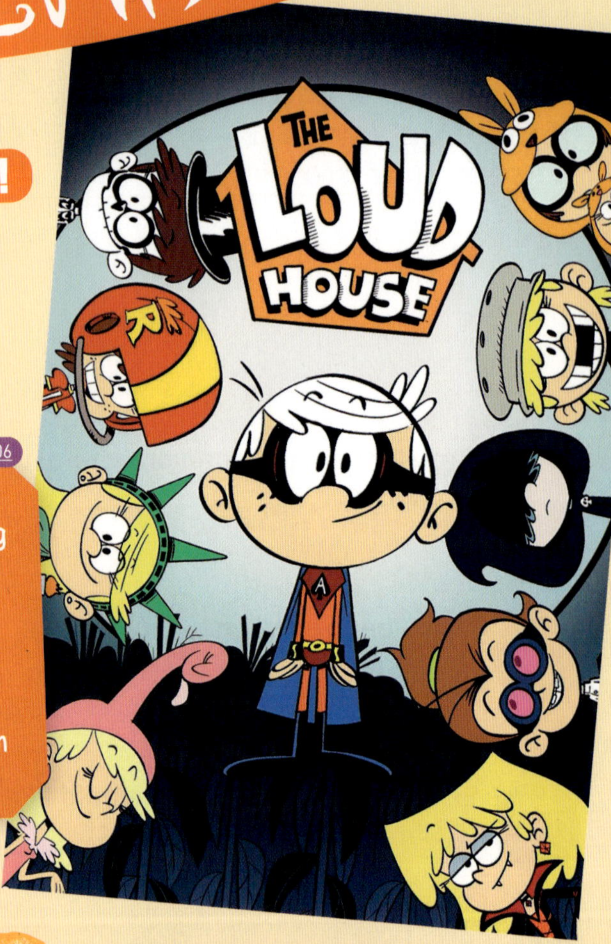

B Trick or treat

1. Listen and repeat.
   Prof 107 Elève 96
2. **GROUP WORK** Recite the poem to the class, just like a rapper!
3. Say what your favourite food is.

Trick or treat!
Give me something good to eat.
Apples, peaches, tangerines.
Happy happy Halloween.

Trick or treat!
Give me something sweet to eat.
Cookies, chocolate, jelly beans.
Happy happy Halloween.

Trick or treat!
Give me something sour to eat.
Lemons, grapefruits, limes so green.
Happy happy Halloween.

Trick or treat!
Give me something good to eat.
Nuts and candy. Lollipops.
Now it's time for us to stop.

Animated poster & worksheet
hatier-clic.fr/21PYB159

C Let's play Halloween Bingo!

✦ momluck.com

1. Say what the different images represent.
2. Choose three images.
3. Write the words in your copybook.
4. Say 'Bingo!' when they are selected.

Time to celebrate Thanksgiving

A What is Thanksgiving?

Prof 108

Thanksgiving Day is a national holiday in the United States of America and Canada. In the USA everybody celebrates Thanksgiving on the fourth Thursday in November. Americans remember the history of the Pilgrim Fathers, a group of English colonists who sailed to North America aboard the Mayflower, in 1620. The story says that Native Americans helped the Pilgrims when they arrived in the USA. Today everyone gives thanks for this generous help. This is why it is called *Thanks - Giving*.

Read the text.

1. Say who celebrates Thanksgiving.
2. Say who the Native Americans are.
3. Say what you give thanks for.

B Macy's annual Thanksgiving parade

✦ 2019

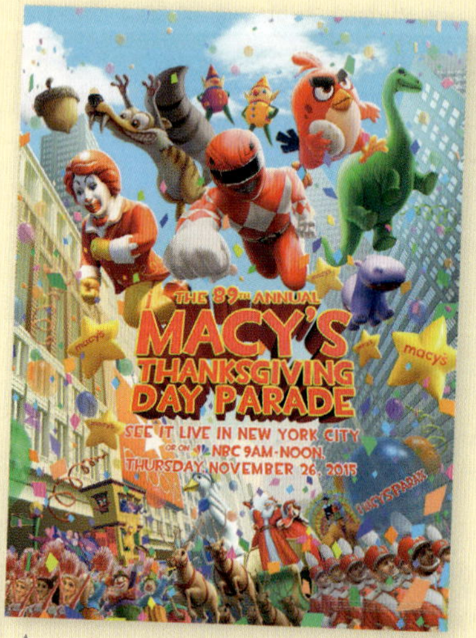

✦ 2015

✦ 2009

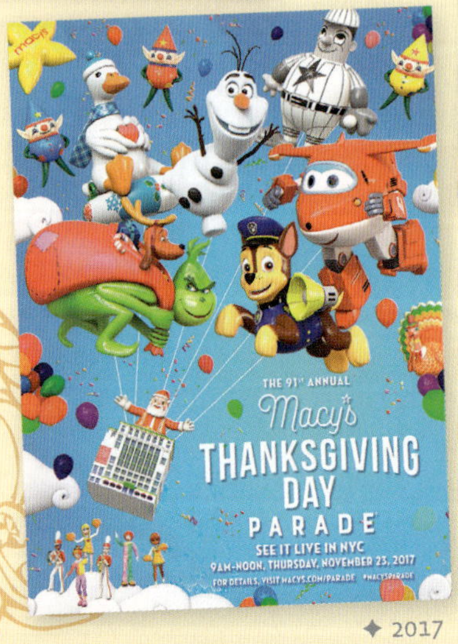

✦ 2017

Look at the different posters.

1. Say who you recognise.
2. Say where they come from.
3. Say what the posters have in common.
4. Imagine a new balloon for the Macy's Parade.

C A little history of the parade

✦ Macy's Thanksgiving Day Parade started small, but keeps growing

1. Give information about the parade.
2. Say who finishes the parade.
3. Imagine a float for this year's parade.

D The Thanksgiving dinner

Norman Rockwell, an American artist, created this painting in November 1942. The painting shows a family at the dinner table. They are preparing to eat the Thanksgiving dinner with lots of turkey and cranberry sauce. This is a very famous painting and there are many funny copies.

✦ This is a famous painting by Norman Rockwell. The name is *Freedom from Want*. It means: "Don't worry, you'll have some food and you'll have a house."

Look at the copies of *Freedom from Want*.

1. Say which characters you recognise.
2. Say where they come from.
3. Say which copy is your favourite.
4. Reimagine the painting with your classmates.

Digital alternative
Create your own painting!

Time to celebrate Christmas

A The Christmas dinner

Point to the different objects. Prof 109

Christmas tree
decorations turkey
carrots Santa hat
Christmas cracker
vegetables presents
star paper hat
lights
roast potatoes
Yorkshire pudding

Digital alternative
Spot the difference!

B Christmas cards

Prof 110

Christmas cards are very important in Great Britain and in North America. People send millions of cards to their friends, family and colleagues. They are an integral part of the Christmas decorations at home. Charities also collect a lot of money selling cards and this money helps to change the lives of many people around the world.

1. Choose a friend and send him or her a Christmas card.
2. Write your special Christmas message.
3. Display all the cards in the classroom.

Animated poster & worksheet
hatier-clic.fr/21PYB163a

C International ugly sweater day

1. Describe the man's sweater then the woman's sweater.
2. Say which one you prefer.
3. Describe your ugly sweater to the class.
4. Organise an "Ugly Sweater Day" in your school.

Everywhere in the world, people do something strange on the 3rd Friday in December. They don't wear their normal clothes. They wear a funny and very ugly pullover to celebrate Christmas. Reindeers! Christmas trees! Elves! Even decorations! Be creative!

Christmas crackers are very popular in the United Kingdom. When you pull the cracker, it goes 'pop!'. Inside there is a paper crown, a 'terrible' joke and a little present.

D Christmas crackers

1. Make your own crackers for your family dinner. Write a kind message.
2. Suggest something for the little present.
3. Try and find a terrible joke!

Father Christmas is married to Mrs Christmas. What's her first name?
Mary! Because... Mary Christmas!' LOL!

What do elves post on Social Media?
Elf-ies!

What do Santa's little helpers learn at school?
The elf-abet!

What do snowmen eat for lunch?
Iceburgers or Brrrr-itos!

What do you call an art museum in an igloo?
The Ig-Louvre!

E Now... let's sing!

hatier-clic.fr/21PYB163b

All I Want for Christmas is youuuuu

✦ Mariah Carey - *All I Want for Christmas Is You*

1. Say what you see in the video.
2. Say the words you understand in the video.
3. Now, sing along. hatier-clic.fr/21PYB163c

✦ *All I Want for Christmas – Lyrics*

Time to celebrate Saint Patrick's Day!

A What is Saint Patrick's Day?

Prof 111

On March 17th people in Ireland and Irish people around the world celebrate this public holiday. Many non-Irish people also enjoy the celebrations, especially in the USA. You can go to festivals and watch parades in cities like New York, Boston, and obviously the Irish capital, Dublin. The city of Chicago puts food colouring into its river. The river goes green!

Read the text.

1. Say who celebrates Saint Patrick's Day.
2. Say where Saint Patrick's Day is celebrated.
3. Say what people do on this day.

B Saint Patrick's Day traditions

1. Watch the video.
2. Say what you understand about Saint Patrick's Day.

Prof 16

✦ St. Patrick's Day Traditions

Animated poster & worksheet
hatier-clic.fr/21PYB165

C Let's go green

1. Say what green clothes you can see in the picture.
2. Say what green clothes you have.
3. **GROUP WORK** Organise Saint Patrick's Day in your school.
4. **PAIR WORK** Do the green scavenger hunt.

Green is the symbolic colour of the day. Lots of people wear green clothes on Saint Patrick's Day: green pullovers, green t-shirts, green trousers, green socks and green shoes.

D Eat your greens

1. Say what food is green.
2. Say what colour these meals normally are.
3. Learn how to make green pasta.

People change the colour of their food. They don't just eat green vegetables, but they do have green hot dogs, green cookies, green pancakes, green pasta and green drinks.

Time to be at school

Trip 1

School

1 school badge
2 blazer
3 blouse
4 skirt
5 tights
6 shoes
7 trousers
8 shirt
9 desk
10 crayons
11 scissors
12 glue
13 map
14 pencils
15 paper
16 bin
17 book
18 notebook
19 ruler
20 pen

Time to help the others

Trip 2

Superheroes

1 help
2 fly
3 save
4 face
5 nose
6 mouth
7 ears
8 hair (curly/straight/long/short)
9 eyes
10 small
11 costume
12 belt
13 cloak
14 mask
15 gloves

Time to cook

Trip 3

Food

1 flour
2 eggs
3 milk
4 bowl
5 whisk
6 crack
7 chicken
8 broccoli
9 tomatoes
10 peas
11 cut
12 dish
13 fridge
14 cooker
15 saucepan

Time to celebrate with the family

Trip 4

Family

1 grandmother
2 grandfather
3 father
4 mother
5 sister
6 brother
7 cousin
8 uncle
9 aunt
10 tablecloth
11 plate
12 glass
13 spoon
14 gift
15 scrap paper chain

Time to stay at home Trip 5

House

1. house
2. garden
3. bedroom
4. living-room
5. dining-room
6. bathroom
7. kitchen
8. couch
9. armchair
10. tv set
11. computer
12. bookshelves
13. read
14. watch tv
15. brush your teeth
16. work

Time to play

Trip 6

Let's play

1 playground
2 play soccer
3 play basketball
4 hang out with friends
5 court
6 bench
7 swings
8 shelter
9 hopscotch
10 scooter
11 roller skates
12 bike
13 cycle
14 run
15 skipping rope
16 big wheel
17 roundabout

Trip 7 Time to dress up

Monsters

1 witch
2 werewolf
3 vampire
4 ghost
5 wig
6 cloak
7 claws
8 fur
9 fangs
10 wand
11 pumpkin
12 spider
13 black cat
14 growl
15 laugh

Time to visit London

Trip 8

London

1. Tube
2. double decker bus
3. black cab
4. boat
5. river Thames
6. phone booth
7. park
8. bridge
9. clock
10. street
11. car
12. river banks
13. visit
14. street lamp
15. museum

Time to think green

Trip 9

Plastic

1. sort
2. reduce
3. reuse
4. recycle
5. single use plastic
6. cup
7. straw
8. plastic bag
9. tote bag
10. ceramic cup
11. refillable bottle
12. reusable lunch box
13. cardboard box
14. soda can
15. water bottle

Time to imagine your future job

Trip 10

Inventors

1 fireman
2 nurse
3 scientist
4 plumber
5 mechanic
6 policeman
7 vet
8 businessman
9 mayor
10 secretary
11 speak
12 phone
13 listen
14 drink
15 write

4 h ph © Nancy Honey / www.agefotostock.com / **4** b ph © art copyright Dan Avenell / **5** h ph © Carmen Valiño / **5** b ph © Chris Jackson / Handout / Buckingham Palace via Getty Images via AFP / **6** h ph © Jason Cameron / **6** b ph © Marmaduke St. John / Alamy Stock Photo / **7** h ph © ® Digital image, The Museum of Modern Art, New York / Scala, Florence / © Tim Burton / **7** b © Vicky Scott / **8** h ph © Wavebreak Media Ultra / www.agefotostock.com / **8** b Coll. Christophel © Aardman Animations / **14** ph © Syda Productions / Shutterstock / **15** h ph © fuwari / iStock / Getty Images Plus / **15** m ph © arta / Shutterstock / **15** bg1 ph © Tania Bondar / iStock / Getty Images Plus / **15** bg2 ph © the8monkey / iStock / Getty Images Plus / **15** bg3 ph © shaitan1985 / stock.adobe.com / **15** bg4 ph © Terriana / iStock / Getty Images Plus / **15** bm ph © d1sk / iStock / Getty Images Plus / **17** h1 ph © Sergei Krestinin / iStock / Getty Images Plus / **17** h2 ph © Olga Kurbatova / iStock / Getty Images Plus / **17** h3 ph © Oceloti / iStock / Getty Images Plus / **17** h4 ph © sabelskaya / iStock / Getty Images Plus / **17** b ph © Bananaboy / Shutterstock / **18** ph © Getting Lost On Your First Day of School I Our School © Twofour © ITN Source/ITV Studios / **18** -19 ph © Nancy Honey / www.agefotostock.com / **21** h ph © AJ_Watt / E+ / Getty Images / **21** b © Created by Jane Leigh of Tytherington School / **22** h1 ph © Irina Qiwi / Shutterstock / **22** h2 ph © Alexkava / stock.adobe.com / **22** h3 ph © diamondtetra / stock.adobe.com / **22** h4 ph © jeksonjs / stock.adobe.com / **22** b ph © Warner Bros / BBQ_DFY / Aurimages / **23** ph © Friendship Soup © Clarke Media, D.R. / **28** g ph © Monkey Business Images / Shutterstock / **28** d © Living Streets, the UK charity for everyday walking / **29** h1,b6 ph © Ольга Погорелова / stock.adobe.com / **29** h2,b2 ph © piai / stock.adobe.com / **29** h3,b4 ph © Dmitriy Kazitsyn / stock.adobe.com / **29** h4,m5 ph © Paulista / stock.adobe.com / **29** h5,m3 ph © Xana_UKR / Shutterstock / **29** h6 ph © viktorijareut / stock.adobe.com / **29** m1,b3 ph © Roman Dekan / stock.adobe.com / **29** m2,b1 ph © chrupka / stock.adobe.com / **29** m4 ph © bohbeh / stock.adobe.com / **29** m6 ph © Suraphol / stock.adobe.com / **29** b5 ph © ankomando / Shutterstock / **30** h ph © Wordley Calvo Stock / stock.adobe.com / **30** -1 ph © denis_pc / stock.adobe.com / **30** -2 ph © lisima / stock.adobe.com / **30** -3 ph © Colorfuel Studio / stock.adobe.com / **30** -4 ph © Lorelyn Medina / stock.adobe.com / **30** -5 ph © YummyBuum / stock.adobe.com / **30** -6,7 ph © EvgeniyBobrov / stock.adobe.com / **31** ph © Stephen Simpson / DigitalVision / Getty Images / **32** -33 © art Dan Avenell / **34** b © 2021 Marvel Characters, Inc. / D.R. / **35** From Dog Man and Cat Kid by Dav Pilkey. Copyright © 2017 by Dav Pilkey. Reprinted by permission of Scholastic Inc. / **36** © Thomas Krajewski and Jennifer Muro (art: Gretel Lusky) / DC Comics, 2020 / D.R. / **37** ph © D.R. / **38** © From Dog Man #1 by Dav Pilkey. Copyright © 2017 by Dav Pilkey. Reprinted by permission of Scholastic / **39** h ph © 2021 Marvel Characters, Inc. / D.R. / **42** g ph © Banksy / **42** d ph © Ben Turnbull / **43** -1 ph © Warner Bros. / AF archive / Alamy Stock Photo / **43** -2,3 ph © DC Comics / D.R. / **43** -4 ph © 2021 Marvel Characters, Inc. / D.R. / **43** -5 ph © Warner Bros./ Everett Collection / Bridgeman Images / **43** -6 ph © Rob Liefeld / Marvel Comics / D.R. / **43** -7,8 ph © 2021 Marvel Characters, Inc. / D.R. / **43** -9 ph © DC Comics / D.R. / **43** -10,11 ph © 2021 Marvel Characters, Inc. / D.R. / **43** -12 ph © DC Comics / D.R. / **43** -13,14 ph © 2021 Marvel Characters, Inc. / D.R. / **43** -15 ph © Bridgeman Images / **44** ph © Ollie Millington / Getty Images / **45** ph © durantelallera / stock.adobe.com / **46** ph © Sydney International Food Festival, 2014. Australia © Garry Horner (Creative director), Natalie Boog (photographer) © Whybin / TBWA / **46** -47 ph © Carmen Valiño / **48** -1,2 ph © Joe Gough / stock.adobe.com / **48** -3 ph © cdkproductions / stock.adobe.com / **49** hg Kids try australian snacks I Kids Vs. Food © FBE, D.R. / **49** hd ph © sheilaf2002 / stock.adobe.com / **49** bg ph © Sudowoodo / Shutterstock / **49** bdh ph © Dima / stock.adobe.com / **49** bdb ph © silanti / Shutterstock / **50** -1 ph © Tap10 / stock.adobe.com / **50** -2 ph © Courtesy of @helloberryworld / **50** -3 ph © Aiselin82 / iStock / Getty Images Plus / **51** h ph © TorriPhoto / Shutterstock / **51** b1 ph © Anton Ignatenco / stock.adobe.com / **51** b2 ph © Cindy Creighton / Shutterstock / **51** b3 ph © Baiba Opule / stock.adobe.com / **56** h ph © Sarah Rosado / **56** b ph © Image copyright and courtesy of James Ostrer / **57** h ph © Le Hobbit - un voyage inattendu (2012) - Dir: Peter Jackson / New Line Cinema / The Kobal Collection / Aurimages / **57** m Coll. Christophel © Warner Bros. / Heyday Films / **57** b "Matilda: The Chocolate Cake Edition" © Roald Dahl (Author), Quentin Blake (illustration) / © Puffin Books, 2019 / **59** ph © Imgorthand / E+/ Getty Images / **60** -61 ph © Chris Jackson / Handout / Buckingham Palace via Getty Images via AFP / **62** hd ph © mona redshinestudio / Shutterstock / **62** ph © Chris Jackson / Handout / Clarence House via Getty Images via AFP / **63** h ph © Andy Clark / Reuters / **63** b Coll. Christophel © Belga Productions - nWave Pictures / **64** Coll. Christophel © Netflix / EH Productions / Legendary Entertainment / PCMA Productions / Warner Bros. / **65** h,b Coll. Christophel © Netflix / EH Productions / Legendary Entertainment / PCMA Productions / Warner Bros. / **66** g ph © Alpha Press / Maxppp / **66** d ph © Chris Jackson / Chris Jackson Collection / Getty Images via AFP / **67** Coll. Christophel © Robert Viglaski / Netflix / EH Productions / Legendary Entertainment / PCMA Productions / Warner Bros. / **70** h ph © Pictorial Press Ltd / Alamy Stock Photo / **70** b ph © Jeff Kravitz / FilmMagic, Inc / Getty Images / **71** fond Doc. Henriette Vivien / **71** hg "Charlie and the Chocolate Factory" / © Roald Dahl (Author), Quentin Blake (Illustrations) / © Puffin Books, 2007 / **71** hd ph © Christophel © Warner Bros / **71** bg ph © Warner Bros. / The Kobal Collection / Mountain, Peter / Aurimages / **71** bd ph © "Harry Potter and the Philosopher's Stone" © Bloomsbury Publishing PLC, 1997 / **72** ph © Chris Jackson / Getty Images / **73** ph © SDI Productions / E+ / Getty Images / **74** -75 ph © Jason Cameron / **76** Coll. Christophel © Geffen Company / Warner Bros. / **77** h1 ph © agsaz / Shutterstock / **77** h2 ph © Terraxplorer / E+ / Getty Images / **77** h3 ph © Alexander Spatari / Moment / Getty Images / **78** h,b Coll. Christophel © Nickelodeon Animation Studios/ CANAL + / **79** h,b Coll. Christophel © Nickelodeon Animation Studios/ CANAL + / **84** ph © Carson Ellis (Author, Illustrations) / © Walker Books Ltd, 2016 / **86** ph © korisbo / Shutterstock / **87** ph © Mollymoocraft / **88** -89 ph © Marmaduke St. John / Alamy Stock Photo / **90** h ph © Justin Sullivan / Getty Images / AFP / **90** b ph © Richard Levine / Alamy Stock Photo / **91** h ph © Recess Activities © Totowa Broadcast News, D.R. / **91** bg1 ph © Colorcocktail / Shutterstock / **91** bg2 ph © MicroOne / Shutterstock / **91** bg3 ph © Archimicrostock / stock.adobe.com / **91** bd ph © Frances Roberts / Alamy Stock Photo / **92** ph © "Playground Problem" by Margaret McNamara (Author), Mike Gordon (Illustrations) / © Simon Spotlight, 2004 / **93** h ph © "Ian" by Mundoloco, © CGI Ian Foundation © TheCGBros / **93** b ph © Boys & Girls Clubs of Santa Fe / Del Norte / **98** h ph © Howie Green / www.howiegreen.com / **98** b ph © Thomas Buxton Primary School / **99** ph © Zorica Lukacev - Gra / stock.adobe.com / **100** h ph © Peter Cade / Getty Images / **100** b ph © clubfoto / istock / Getty Images / **101** ph © Marmaduke St. John / Alamy Stock Photo / **102** -103 ph © ® Digital image, The Museum of Modern Art, New York / Scala, Florence / © Tim Burton / **104** "A Babysitter's Guide to Monster Hunting" by Rachel Talalay / ph © Netflix / BBQ_DFY / Aurimages / **105** h ph © Clipart-Library / **105** b1 ph © Visual Generation / Shutterstock / **105** b2,3 ph © vectorkif / stock.adobe.com / **106** -107h ph © "How to Make Friends With a Ghost" by Rebecca Green (2017) / Tundra Books - Penguin Random House Canada Young Readers / **107** b ph © Rebecca Green / Tundra Books - Penguin Random House Canada Young Readers / **111** ph © ProStockStudio / Shutterstock / **112** ph © Jasper St Aubyn West (Tail Jar) / **114** ph © Walt Disney / Pixar / BBQ_DFY / Aurimages / **115** ph © Jemal Countess / Getty Images / AFP / © Tim Burton / MoMa, New York / **116** -117 ph © Vicky Scott / **118** ph © Kids View: What to do in London (Insider tips from local kids) © Family Travel, familytravel.com.au, D.R. / **119** h ph © rsaraiva / iStock / Getty Images Plus / **119** mg © The Royal Parks / www.royalparks.org.uk / **119** mh ph © Kolonko / Shutterstock / **119** mdh ph © chrisdorney / iStock / Getty Images Plus / **119** mdb ph © one2tim / iStock / Getty Images Plus / **120** h1 ph © Allstar Picture Library Ltd. / Alamy Stock Photo / © Studiocanal / **120** h2 Coll. Christophel © Hartswood Films / **120** h3 ph © Jay Maidment / Walt Disney / Kobal / REX / Shutterstock / Aurimages / **120** b-a ph © Amelia Lola / @machodoodle / **120** b-b ph © Yottoy / D.R. / **120** b-c1 ph © Julija / stock.adobe.com / **120** b-c2 ph © Aleksandra Smirnova / stock.adobe.com / **121** h,b Coll. Christophel © Hartswood Films 2012 / **123** bd ph © ChoochartSansong / iStock / Getty Images Plus / **125** g ph © Thames river cruises / Headout UK Ltd. / **125** d ph © topvectors / stock.adobe.com / **126** h ph © Iain Masterton / Alamy Stock Photo / **126** m ph © William Hook (from Stafford, United Kingdom) Creative Commons Attribution-Share Alike 2.0 Generic / **126** b ph © Kamira / Shutterstock / **127** h1 ph © d3images © darius.l / stock.adobe.com / **127** h2 ph © fkprojects / stock.adobe.com / **127** -1 ph © Eugene Sergeev / stock.adobe.com / **127** -2 ph © AbleStock.com / Getty Images Plus / **127** -3 ph © Panagiotis Kotsovolos / Alamy Stock Photo / **127** -5 ph © Victor Huang / iStock / Getty Images Plus / **127** -6 ph © Yuri Turkov / Alamy Stock Photo / **127** -7 ph © ChrisSteer / E+ / Getty Images / **127** -8 ph © Julio Etchart / Alamy Stock Photo / **127** -10 ph © oversnap / iStock / Getty Images Plus / **127** -11 ph © william87 / iStock / Getty Images Plus / **127** -13 ph © Carol Yepes / Moment Open / Getty Images / **127** -15 ph © Alex Segre / Moment Mobile / Getty Images / **127** -18 ph © William Hook (from Stafford, United Kingdom) Creative Commons Attribution-Share Alike 2.0 Generic / **127** -20 ph © 400tmax / iStock / Getty Images Plus / **127** -22 ph © Kamira / Shutterstock / **127** -23 ph © borchee / iStock / Getty Images Plus / **127** -24 ph © Greenwich National Maritime Museum, UK / ph © Leemage/Corbis via Getty Images / **127** -27 ph © Allan Baxter / The Image Bank / Getty Images / **127** -28 ph © Olaf Krüger / imageBROKER / Alamy Stock Photo / **127** -30 ph © Vladislav Zolotov / iStock / Getty Images Plus / **127** signs ph © Даша Мельник / stock.adobe.com / **128** h1 ph © AbleStock.com / Getty Images Plus / **128** h2 ph © Allan Baxter / The Image Bank / Getty Images / **128** h3 ph © Julio Etchart / Alamy Stock Photo / **128** h4 ph © Imagepast / Alamy Stock Photo / **128** b © Base map © maproom.net / **129** ph © Vladislav Zolotov / iStock / Getty Images Plus / **130** -131 ph © Wavebreak Media Ultra / www.agefotostock.com / **132** ph © Nottingham Post / Reach Picture / **133** h ph © Fabio De Paola / Shutterstock / **133** b ph © Lexi's Clean Living / **134** ph © Westend61 / Nico Hermann / Getty Images / **135** b ph © happiestsim - stock.adobe.com / **139** ph © Tatyana Khromova / Shutterstock / **140** h ph © James Beck / Alamy Stock Photo / © Sue Lipscombe / **140** b ph © WashedAshore.org / **141** h ph © Birth Brand / Shutterstock / **142** h ph © Shane Woodward / **142** b ph © The 3R's / **143** ph © Robert Meyers / Alamy Stock Photo / **144** -145 Coll. Christophel © Aardman Animations / **146** « Big hero 6 », 2015. Coll. Christophel © FortyFour Studios / Walt Disney Animation Studios / **147** h ph © Illustrations 2015 Andrew Rae / Laurence King Publishing / **147** b ph © boscorelli / Shutterstock / **148** ph © Rachel Murray / Getty Images via AFP / **149** h ph © Official Project I AM / **149** m1 ph © Flashon Studio / Shutterstock / **149** m2 ph © motortion / stock.adobe.com / **149** m3 ph © Africa Studio / stock.adobe.com / **149** m4 ph © AS Photo Project / stock.adobe.com / **149** b1 ph © Andrey_Popov / Shutterstock / **149** b2 ph © Steklo_Krd / stock.adobe.com / **149** b3 ph © Thanagon / stock.adobe.com / **149** b4 ph © Irina / stock.adobe.com / **154** h ph © Mark Rigney / Hookedblog.co.uk / © Dave the chimp / **154** b ph © Courtesy of Dave The Chimp / **155** h ph © Feng Yu / stock.adobe.com / **155** b ph © borzebra / stock.adobe.com / **157** ph © The Children's Museum of Indianapolis / **158** h Coll. Christophel © Nickelodeon Animation Studios/ CANAL + / **158** b ph © Sergey Novikov / Shutterstock / **159** ph © momluck.com / **160** h ph © Aleutie / Shutterstock / **160** b ph © Macy's Thanksgiving Day Parade © 2021 Macy's, Inc. All Rights Reserved / **161** h ph © Macy's, Inc. / **161** m1 ph © Charles Boyer / Walt Disney, 1993 / **161** m2 "The Simpsons", by Matt Groening. 2019. S 31 ep 8 : Thanksgiving of Horror Animation / ph © 20th Century Fox Television / BBQ_DFY / Aurimages / **161** m3 ph © Musée Norman Rockwell, Stockbridge (Massachusetts) © Printed by permission of the Norman Rockwell Family Agency Copyright ©1943 the Norman Rockwell Family Entities / **161** b ph © Grégory Litré / **162** h ph © dglimages / stock.adobe.com / **162** b ph © incamerastock / Alamy Stock Photo / **163** h ph © Roman Samborskyi / Shutterstock / **163** m ph © WavebreakMediaMicro / stock.adobe.com / **163** b ph © Jeff Kravitz / FilmMagic for Mariah Carey / Getty Images / **164** hg ph © Yannick Tylle / Corbis Documentary / Getty Images / **164** hd ph © Jill Brady / Portland Portland Press Herald via Getty Images / **164** mg ph © Brian Lawless/ PA Images / Alamy Stock Photo / **164** md ph © Paul Faith / AFP / **164** b ph © St. Patrick's Day Traditions © pocketpassport.com / **165** h ph © JoeFoxBerlin / Radharc Images / Alamy Stock Photo / **165** -1 ph © manyakotic / stock.adobe.com / **165** -2 ph © vm2002 / stock.adobe.com / **165** -3 ph © yuliiaholovchenko / stock.adobe.com / **165** -4 ph © G. Martysheva / Shutterstock / **165** fond ph © Jiri Hera / stock.adobe.com

D.R. : Malgré nos efforts, il nous a été impossible de joindre certains auteurs ou leurs ayants-droit pour solliciter l'autorisation de reproduction, nous avons réservé en notre comptabilité les droits usuels.

Iconographie : Véronique Foz

IMPRIM'VERT®

Achevé d'imprimer en France par Pollina - 13238
Dépôt légal : 07721-8/01 - Avril 2021

PAPIER À BASE DE FIBRES CERTIFIÉES

Hatier s'engage pour l'environnement en réduisant l'empreinte carbone de ses livres. Celle de cet exemplaire est de : 950 g éq. CO_2
Rendez-vous sur www.hatier-durable.fr

RUSSIA
ALASKA
CANADA
Juneau
CANADA
Olympia
WASHINGTON
Salem
OREGON
Boise
IDAHO
Helena
MONTANA
WYOMING
Cheyenne
Bismarck
NORTH DAKOTA
SOUTH DAKOTA
Pierre
NEBRASKA
Lincoln
MINNESOTA
St. Paul
WISCONSIN
Madison
MICHIGAN
Lansing
IOWA
Des Moines
ILLINOIS
Springfield
INDIANA
Indianapolis
OHIO
Columbus
PENNSYLVANIA
Harrisburg
NEW YORK
Albany
VERMONT
Montpelier
MAINE
Augusta
NEW HAMPSHIRE
Concord
MASSACHUSETTS
Boston
RHODE ISLAND
Providence
Hartford
CONNECTICUT
Trenton
NEW JERSEY
Dover
DELAWARE
Annapolis
MARYLAND
WEST VIRGINIA
Charleston
Richmond
VIRGINIA
Raleigh
NORTH CAROLINA
Columbia
SOUTH CAROLINA
Atlanta
GEORGIA
FLORIDA
Tallahassee
Montgomery
ALABAMA
Jackson
MISSISSIPPI
Baton Rouge
LOUISIANA
Little Rock
ARKANSAS
TENNESSEE
Nashville
KENTUCKY
Frankfort
MISSOURI
Jefferson City
KANSAS
Topeka
Oklahoma City
OKLAHOMA
TEXAS
Austin
NEW MEXICO
Santa Fe
COLORADO
Denver
UTAH
Salt Lake City
ARIZONA
Phoenix
NEVADA
Carson City
CALIFORNIA
Sacramento
HOLLYWOOD
MEXIQUE
Honolulu
HAWAII

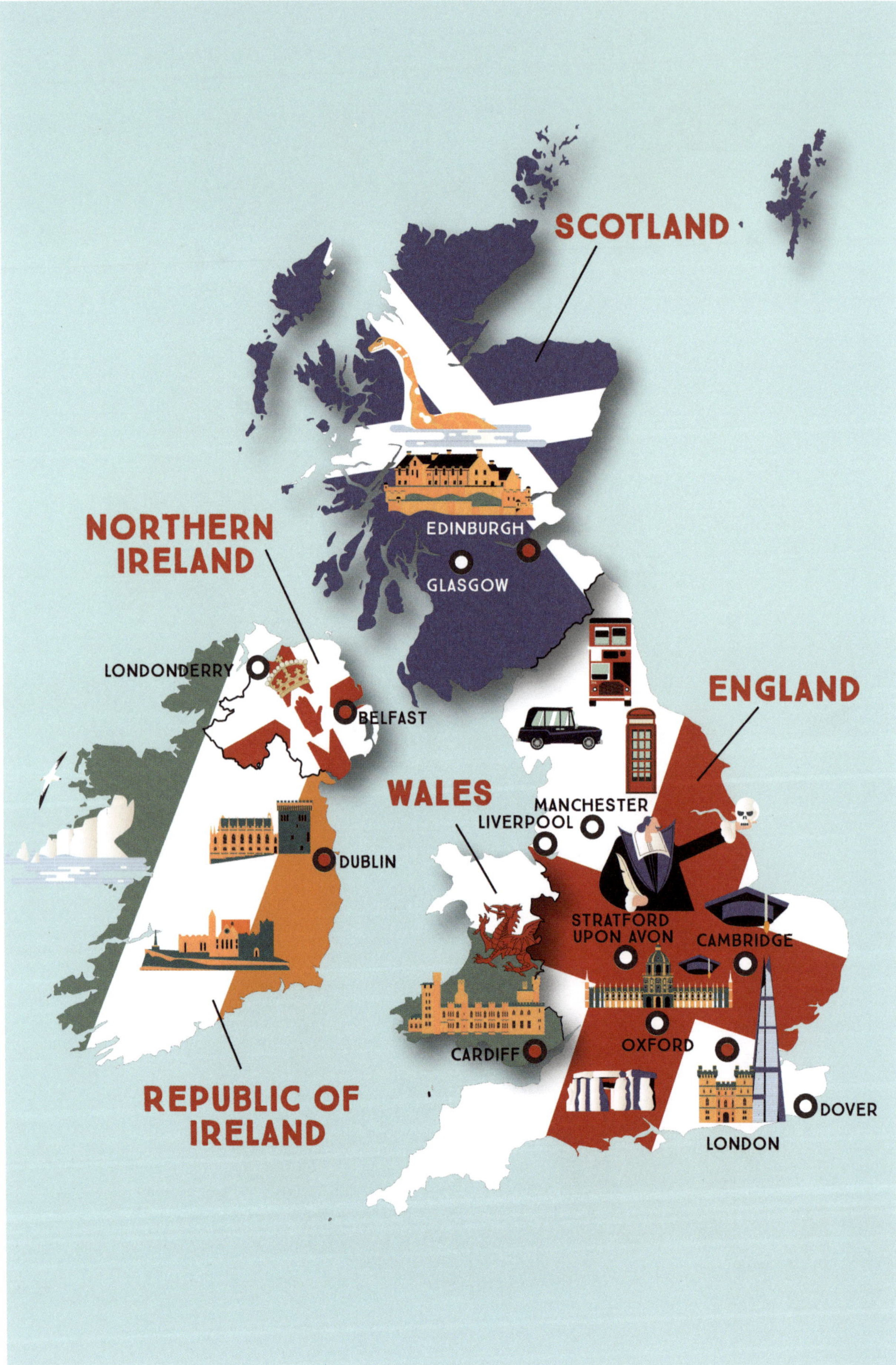
SCOTLAND
NORTHERN IRELAND
EDINBURGH
GLASGOW
LONDONDERRY
BELFAST
ENGLAND
WALES
MANCHESTER
LIVERPOOL
DUBLIN
STRATFORD UPON AVON
CAMBRIDGE
OXFORD
CARDIFF
DOVER
LONDON
REPUBLIC OF IRELAND